LETTING GO OF YOUR PAST

ED TAYLOR

HARVEST HOUSE PUBLISHERS
EUGENE, OREGON

The information presented in this book is meant to be used for general resource purposes only. It is not intended to serve as a mental health or medical guide, nor should it substitute medical advice from a health care professional. If you have or think you may have a medical problem, speak to your doctor or health care practitioner immediately about your risk and possible treatments. Do not engage in any therapy or treatment without consulting a mental health or medical professional.

Cover design by Studio Gearbox

Cover images © Rita Soni / Shutterstock

Interior design by KUHN Design Group

For bulk, special sales, or ministry purchases, please call 1-800-547-8979.
Email: CustomerService@hhpbooks.com

Letting Go of Your Past

Published by Harvest House Publishers
Eugene, Oregon 97408
www.harvesthousepublishers.com

ISBN 978-0-7369-9208-4 (pbk)
ISBN 978-0-7369-9209-1 (eBook)

Library of Congress Control Number: 2024952801

Printed in the United States of America

25 26 27 28 29 30 31 32 33 / BP / 10 9 8 7 6 5 4 3 2 1

ACKNOWLEDGMENTS

My life's ministry and this book are dedicated to Jesus Christ.

I'm especially grateful for my wife Marie and kids, Joshua and Caitlin, with deep memories of our son Eddie and his son, our grandson Levi (#onedaylittleguy).

This book is for all those crippled by their past, tainted by sin, but hopeful for change. God is ready to work deeply in your heart, mind, and soul! Trust Him.

Thank you, Catherine McDaugale for the investment of time in helping me edit these Bible studies into a readable book format.

Thank you, Marie, Tonya, and Julie for your proofreading and suggestions.

Thank you, pastors Skip Heitzig, Chuck Smith, Jeff Johnson, Greg Laurie, Warren Wiersbe, and so many others, who have taught and mentored me through your ministries.

And a *huge* thank you to the fellowship family of Calvary Church, whose love and support mean so much to us.

There is therefore now no condemnation to those who are in Christ Jesus, who do not walk according to the flesh, but according to the Spirit.

ROMANS 8:1

CONTENTS

Foreword by Joel C. Rosenberg 9

1. We All Have a Past 11

2. Dealing with Condemnation 17

3. Dealing with the Law of God 35

4. Dealing with Your Past 53

5. Dealing with Forgiveness 75

6. Dealing with Your Anger 95

7. Dealing with the Present 121

8. Dealing with Spiritual Warfare and the Devil 141

9. Dealing with Spiritual Warfare—How to Wage the Battle . . . 159

10. Dealing with Your Identity 177

Afterword 197

Notes 199

FOREWORD

Joel C. Rosenberg

Ed Taylor is a dear friend, a loving and compassionate husband and father, and a wise and fruitful pastor and Bible teacher.

But it was not always so.

Ed has a past—and not a good one.

During the years of our friendship, Ed has been courageously and refreshingly candid with me about his life before Jesus Christ saved him.

He's been honest with me about his life before the Lord gave him a hunger for the Word of God, before the Lord drew him into a solid Bible-believing church fellowship, before the Holy Spirit revealed to him the cost to himself and to his lovely wife, Marie, and to their kids the wrong and selfish and destructive choices that he'd been making in his youth.

It's not a pretty picture—with one beautiful exception: When I began to really understand Ed's painful past, I could not help but to rejoice in the power of God's grace and mercy. Because I could see just how radically the Lord has transformed Ed into the humble, kind, wise, and servant-hearted husband, father, shepherd, and friend that he is today.

The more I've learned about Ed's past, the more I love the Ed I know today—and the more I love the God who saved him, who saved me too.

To be clear: This book does not contain Ed's testimony.

Rather, it's a book that shares the very important and practical truths that Ed has learned over the years about how to trust the Lord to not get trapped and condemned by his past, but to walk in the freedom and joy and power of the Holy Spirit.

And that is why this book is going to be a great and helpful guide to so many who need to let go of their past as well.

I was so grateful when Ed sent me an advance manuscript copy of this book. So honored that he asked me to write a foreword. And so encouraged when I was able to make the time to read it cover to cover and see the immense eternal blessing it's going to be to everyone who reads it and applies the biblical principles it contains to their own lives.

Just one request: When you finish reading it and find yourself similarly blessed, please don't keep this treasure to yourself. Give a copy to family members and friends who are struggling with feelings of guilt and condemnation for choices they had made in their past and needing to find the healing power of Christ's full and forever forgiveness.

Thanks, and may the Lord God bless you as you let go of your past and embrace His beautiful plan and purpose for your future.

I know the plans I have for you, declares the LORD, plans for welfare and not for evil, to give you a future and a hope.

JEREMIAH 29:11 (ESV)

1

WE ALL HAVE A PAST

Are you being taunted by your past? Do you feel condemned by the things you've done or by what has happened to you? If so, this is something you really need to hear. The Bible teaches us,

> There is therefore now *no condemnation to those who are in Christ Jesus*, who do not walk according to the flesh, but according to the Spirit (Romans 8:1, emphasis added).

Did you catch that? You are not condemned if you're in Christ. In Christ is a great place to be.

- In Christ, your sin has been judged. The penalty has been paid by Jesus.
- In Christ, your sins have been forgiven and washed away. Your sins have been blotted out like a thick cloud (Isaiah 44:22). Blotted out; gone.
- In Christ, God hasn't dealt with you according to your iniquities. He has removed your sins as far as the east is from the west (Psalm 103:10, 12).

- In Christ, your sins have been cast into the depths of the sea (Micah 7:19).

It is great to be in Christ.

But you can sense there still remains a problem in your life. You have a past. It's like a shadow, a cloud that follows you around. You can tell yourself there's no condemnation because you're in Christ. But what should you do with your past now that you know that truth?

We all have a past, pasts that can mock and plague us. Ones that shoot arrows of condemnation at us. Our pasts try to undermine our faith. And our pasts follow us around wherever we go.

For example, let's consider music. It doesn't matter where you go today, '80s music can be heard playing in the background in many places. You could be in the supermarket, the mall, the doctor's office, the elevator—it's everywhere. You can't get away from it.

While '80s music may mean nothing to you, it means a lot to me and has an effect inside me. It takes me back to the 1980s. I need to let you know that the '80s was when I did the most damage to my life and to the lives of other people around me. There are certain episodes in my life that are tied to songs. When particular songs come on the radio, it takes me right back to specific days in my memory. I may not have thought about an event in 15 years, but when I hear certain songs, I'm right back there.

And that's happened to me quite a few times. I have needed to make a conscious decision in my life that I'm not stuck in the '80s anymore. Isn't that great? I have needed to tell myself: I don't live in the '80s. It's true. Today is the day of salvation. Today is the day that Jesus has redeemed me and changed me. Now, I don't care if I hear those goofy songs anymore. I'm not in the '80s. God has changed my life. The Ed of the '80s is dead.

It's the same for all of us. There are all sorts of reminders that are trying to drag you back to your past. Thoughts. Memories. Pictures.

The enemy has your number. He knows that you've tied a connection from a situation in your life to a specific song, scent, place, person, or whatever else. Satan knows that.

The situation is constantly being presented before you because the enemy knows that, if he can get you to look backward, you'll be stuck. And when you're stuck, you're not moving forward. You're only going down. And so, he wants to pull you back.

Now, your past might not be as bad as mine. My past might not be as bad as yours. But we all have a past. And you likely have something in your life that you would wipe away if you had the chance. If you could, you would permanently erase it. For many, it's a constant shadow in their life.

I know I'm not proud of my past. There's a lot that I wish I would have avoided. I don't like it. At some time, you've likely asked yourself that popular philosophical question: *If you could do anything to change your past, would you do it?* My answer is of course! I would want to avoid a lot of my pain that has been caused by sin. I wouldn't want to hurt people like I did.

But at the same time, I'm who I am today as a culmination of my past. So if changing my past meant not being where I am today, then the answer is no. It's a trick question. The answer, in truth, is to accept my life as from the Lord.

Sure, I wish a big portion of it wasn't there. But my past is a testimony that God has done an amazing work. There's no question that God has done a work in my life.

I don't know what's in your past. You may have had a very difficult past and made some bad choices. Or you may have taken a relatively moral path and chose to do the right thing most of the time even before you came to Christ.

Regardless of what is in your past, we're all touched by sin. We all have difficulties. Whether you grew up in a hopeless situation or were raised in a godly home, the enemy will use your past against you. The enemy will bring up the way your dad treated you, the way your mom spoke to you, or the way you treated people. Your past has a way of following you.

I remember the first time my past was used against me. Years ago, I had made mistakes while under the influence and I had a criminal record from those mistakes. I applied for a job and the organization ran a background check. When I was asked about my record, I told the administrator that I was a born-again Christian and didn't live that way anymore. But he said, "Well, we don't hire thieves here." And that was it. He didn't even give me a chance.

It was devastating. It was a reminder that although God is quick to forgive us and forget our sins, our world is not so quick to forgive or forget. And we're not always so quick to forgive ourselves.

As your past follows you, you'll need to learn how to navigate your world as a believer in Jesus Christ, even if some of the navigation is only in your own mind. You can enjoy freedom from a past that follows you, taunts you, and even condemns you.

Although you can't change your past, you can hold on to the glorious truth from Romans 8:1. Let's read it again,

> There is therefore *now* no condemnation to those who are in Christ Jesus, who do not walk according to the flesh, but according to the Spirit (emphasis added).

The word *now* in that verse is so important. "There is therefore *now*"—every time you read it, every time you meditate on it, every time you think about it—"no condemnation." Now. *In...this...moment.* Every second of every minute. There is no condemnation for your past. Meditate on this truth.

If you look at this verse in the New King James Version, you'll notice a little asterisk. The asterisk means that the last part of that verse—*who do not walk according to the flesh, but according to the*

Spirit—is present in some, but not all, of the earliest manuscripts that we have of Romans. Even though some manuscripts did not record this phrase in verse 1, we can have confidence in it because it's repeated in Romans 8:4.

You can only fully experience the freedom this truth brings when you're walking in the Spirit. Although you're not condemned as a born-again believer, when you're *not* walking in the Spirit, there are consequences. When you're in the flesh—caught up in yourself and not in the Spirit—you beat yourself up. You heap loads of condemnation on yourself. We don't need someone else to do it for us. We are often our own worst critics.

And even when we *do* walk in the Spirit, there's the challenge of the enemy of our souls who accuses us and tries to condemn us. However, in Christ, there's freedom and safety.

So living with the reality that our past does not go away, a question remains: What do you do with your past?

The good news is that, if you're in Christ—if you're a born-again believer—you don't need to remain in your past. Because there's no condemnation from God, you don't need to be stuck there. You don't need to be trapped or paralyzed by it. You don't need to relive it in your mind on repeat. You don't need to be defined by it.

In Christ, you can move forward. You can live in the present. Jesus has already set you free from your past. You only need to walk in that freedom.

This book will show you how to walk in the freedom that comes from being *in Christ*. You'll learn how to deal with your past through applying biblical wisdom and address the hurt, anger, disappointment, resentment, and regret that consumes you because of the things you've gone through or the things you've done. It's possible to walk in forgiveness and freedom, living moment by moment in Jesus.

REFLECTION/DISCUSSION QUESTIONS

1. What triggers or reminders do you need to surrender to the Lord (like for me, it is music of the '80s) so that the enemy can no longer use them against you?
2. Think about a time in your past that you would really like to erase, but now you can see that the Lord used it powerfully. How did the Lord move in that?
3. What is something from your past that the Lord has forgiven you for, but you still need to forgive yourself for? Do that now; surrender it fully to the Lord.

2

DEALING WITH CONDEMNATION

Condemnation is a heavy and burdensome word. The word condemn means "to declare to be reprehensible, wrong, or evil"; "to pronounce guilty"; to sentence someone; to "doom" someone.[1]

Houses can be condemned. When a house is condemned, it's torn down and never used again. And not only houses, but criminals can be condemned. For them, it means that some will spend many years in prison. Others will never leave prison. *Condemnation* is a heavy word.

Have you ever felt condemned? Have you ever felt like a decision was made against you? Or has someone declared you to be guilty?

Maybe you've experienced this: You are driving down the road, minding your own business, when you notice flashing lights behind you visible in your rearview mirror. You are hoping they are for someone else, but they are for you. You look at the lights. And then, where did your eyes go next? Right to the speedometer.

It's a natural response. Your eyes go to the speedometer and your foot comes off the accelerator. Even if you put your foot on the brakes, it's too late. You're already busted. It makes you feel the same as you did as a kid sitting in the principal's office.

So you pull over. You put your hands on the steering wheel and roll the window down. A police officer comes up to the window of your car and says, "Can I see your driver's license and registration?" You hand the officer what he asked for. As the officer walks away, you wait. You begin to calculate what this infraction will mean for the cost of your insurance and how hard it's going to be to pay the increased rate.

In what seems like an eternity, the officer finally comes back and says, "I'm just going to give you a warning this time. But you know, this area has a lot of kids playing in it, and you need to slow down."

Right then, everything changes. You begin to worship the Lord, "Hallelujah! Thank You, Jesus. What a relief." Now you're going to use cruise control all the way home. You are never going to speed again for the rest of your life.

You know that feeling of relief. Now multiply that by ten billion. Because that's what God's grace has done for us in the spiritual realm. You know you've done wrong. And you know you've made mistakes. You know what you deserve. Yet because of God's grace, you don't get what you deserve. Again, as Paul wrote to the Romans,

> There is therefore now no condemnation to those who are in Christ Jesus, who do not walk according to the flesh, but according to the Spirit (Romans 8:1).

In Christ, there is no condemnation. If you look up the word *no* in Greek, it means "no." But allow me to give you a deeper sense of this word. The word *no* in this verse means no possibility for condemnation. None. Zip. Zero. Nada.

I know the spiritual battle gets heavy sometimes. It's not easy. You get tired of fighting. You no longer want to be waging a battle of the flesh against the Spirit.

In addition, we don't always win our battles. We don't always experience success. It's easy to get caught up in our feelings. And when you're struggling in the realm of feelings, it begins to feel like you'll never make it. It's too much. When you fail—and failure will come to all of us—there's a sense of guilt and shame that can easily lead to self-condemnation.

But for those who are in Christ Jesus, there is no condemnation. Your past sins are forgiven. Your present sins are forgiven. And your future sins are forgiven.

Salvation in Jesus Christ is the whole package. You're not saved one piece of yourself at a time. When a man or a woman is born again, God saves them as a whole package. Your salvation is complete.

God doesn't work within the constraints of time like we do. We live on a linear plane where there is yesterday, today, and tomorrow. But God is outside of time. He lives in the eternal now. And God saves you while knowing everything about you—everything you've ever done and everything you'll ever do.

ARE YOU PRONE TO CONDEMNATION?

Too many Christians—maybe yourself included—live under a sense of condemnation. They think they've done something wrong, and God cannot forgive them. Some go as far to say God *won't* forgive them.

If you're prone to self-condemnation, here are six things to look out for in your life.

1. You always feel guilty.

In your mind, you lean toward the side of assuming guilt. Even when you haven't done anything wrong, you feel guilty. Your guilty conscience never seems to go away.

2. You're often motivated by guilt.

When someone lays a guilt trip on you, you spring into action. It moves you. And even when someone doesn't do this, you do it on your own. You interpret things from a guilty perspective.

3. You're a people pleaser.

You continually look for people to accept, appreciate, notice, and applaud you. When you do well, you expect people to notice and tell you as much. When you don't get that validation from others, you feel bad about yourself. And that feeling is one step away from condemning yourself.

4. You feel like God is mad at you.

Your mistakes continually plague you. When you sit down to read your Bible, you feel like God is mad at you. And when you begin to pray, you feel like God is mad at you. You truly have a sense that God is displeased with you. You may acknowledge that God is not mad with others, but you think He's always angry with you.

5. You never feel like you've done enough.

You could serve in your church for hundreds of hours or pray all night long, but you are still left with a feeling that you should have done more. For example, let's say you make a commitment to go on a five-hour prayer walk. After five hours of walking and praying, instead of being encouraged, you think, *Ah, I could have committed to one more hour*. You beat yourself up because you always feel like you could have or should have done more.

6. You always live in the past.

You live in the past—not in the good parts, but the bad parts. The things that you've done are always on your mind, even if they happened many years ago. You can't stop thinking about them even if they've been long since resolved. You're enslaved by your past.

If you have a tendency toward self-condemnation, what do you do? Start by accepting the fact that if you've asked for forgiveness for your sins—the mistakes you've made—God has forgiven you. The forgiveness of God comes with repentance. And if you are in Christ, there's no condemnation.

HOW TO KNOW IF YOU'RE IN CHRIST

Because there's no condemnation for those who are in Christ, the foundational question concerning your life is: Are you in Christ?

The question is not as hard to answer as it sounds. Let me ask you a different question that you can answer right away. Are you reading this book in your house? That's not a hard question to answer. That is because you know where you are. Either you're in your house, or you're not.

The same holds true when answering the question of whether you're in Christ. You're either in Christ, or you're not. You're either born again into the body of Christ, or you're not.

You may be thinking, *I don't know if I'm in Christ because I blew it this week*. Or maybe you wonder, *I don't know because I've got these negative thoughts*. The mistakes you've made and the thoughts you've had don't affect your position in Christ. You're either born again, or you're not. You're either in Christ, or you're not.

I'm not asking if you were raised in a religious home or if you were baptized as an infant. You're not in Christ simply by going to church on a Sunday morning or because you have attended a church all your life. The question is not asking whether your grandmother was religious or if you've said a prayer here or there. I'm not even asking if you're better than the worst person you can think of.

The question is: Have you been born again? You can be certain you've been born again if you've repented of your sins and acknowledged God as your Creator and His Son Jesus Christ as your Savior—if you've surrendered your life to Him.

Being a born-again believer is a state of surrender. You're no longer living your way. Instead, you want to do things God's way. You won't live perfectly. You'll still make mistakes. But you surrender your life to God.

When you're in Christ Jesus, you're in Him every moment of your life. If you've truly asked Jesus to come into your life and forgive you of your sins—if you've confessed with your mouth the Lord Jesus and believe in your heart that God has raised Him from the dead (Romans 10:9)—you can say that you're in Christ.

THE BENEFITS OF BEING IN CHRIST

Although the Old Covenant (the Law of Moses) was based on what you needed to do to be right with God, the New Covenant (Jesus' redemption) rests on even greater promises. God has given us many promises about who we are in Christ. The benefits of being in Christ are overwhelming. There are at least 90 statements in the Bible about who you are in Christ. Here are just a few of them:

- In Christ, you have been justified freely (Romans 3:24).
- In Christ, you are now dead to sin (Romans 6:11). Sin no longer has the same power over you. This is a very powerful truth. God has given you power, residing inside of you, to live apart from sin. Before you were born again, all you did was sin. You were dead in your trespasses and sin. But now, in Christ, you are dead *to* sin and no longer dead *in* sin.
- In Christ, you have eternal life and the hope of heaven (Romans 6:23).
- In Christ, you will never be separated from the love of God (Romans 8:38-39).
- In Christ, you are part of a new family (Romans 12:5). You've been adopted into a body of believers. It doesn't

matter what separates us from the world's perspective. In Christ, we're one, big family. It doesn't matter where you go in the world or what language you speak. When you are with another believer, you are with family, because we have Jesus in common.

- In Christ, you have confidence. God's promises are true, and He will do what He says He will do (Romans 15:8). Your hope is in Jesus, not in this world. You do not place your hope in government, politics, a president, or a mayor (Daniel 2:21-22). Your hope is not in man. The Bible warns us not to put our trust in man (Psalm 146:3-4).
- In Christ, you have reason to glory, a reason to live (Romans 15:17). You have a purpose to serve and live your life to its fullest.
- In Christ, you are sanctified (1 Corinthians 1:2). That means you've been set apart to be changed. Every single day you live, God is changing you and conforming you into the image of Jesus Christ. Even your worst days are used by God.
- In Christ, God is working all things together for good (Romans 8:28). All of it. Nothing's wasted.
- In Christ, you're a new person—"old things have passed away" and "all things have become new" (2 Corinthians 5:17).

For a list of God's promises about who you are in Christ see chapter 10. All those truths are yours to hold on to. Later, take time to go through each one. You'll be encouraged as you do. At the moment you were born again, you received all of Jesus Christ into your life. And every day since then, you are becoming more conformed into His image.

THE DANGER OF *NOT* BEING IN CHRIST

But for those who aren't in Christ—for those who aren't born again—the Bible paints a stark contrast. It's as clear as black and white. If you don't have Jesus, your life is in spiritual peril. And it's not going to get better. Your life is filled with confusion, guilt, bondage, neglect, and condemnation.

People are hopeless. It's why we're seeing the number of suicides rise to epic proportions. There's nowhere to turn in this world that will give you the satisfaction that comes from Jesus.

We live in a society that calls good, evil and evil, good. Our legislators are making decisions that are hurting society and making things worse. For example, legalizing drugs, like marijuana, won't solve any problems. One of the worst things you can do to a person is to take away the sensitivity and clarity of someone's mind. Marijuana is a gateway drug. It's not the end. It's the beginning of something really, really bad. Making a drug legal doesn't stop it from hurting people.

When you're not in Christ, you can make some really bad decisions. And afterward, you heap loads of condemnation on yourself. By the time someone shared the gospel with me, they didn't need to explain to me the issue of my sin. They didn't need to hand me a list of 100 sins found in the Bible and hope that one of them would hit my soul.

While at the time, I didn't use the word *sin*, I knew about my bad behavior. I was strongly aware of those instances when I would wake up face down somewhere in the city after the effects of the alcohol I consumed the night before wore off. The night prior, I had done something so bad that my friends had pulled the car over, opened the door, and kicked me out.

Apart from Christ, I couldn't get away from my worry and anxiety. After a night of drinking myself into darkness, I would wake up and wonder what I had done. Then, when I found out, I would think, *I just can't believe it. What kind of person am I?*

On one occasion, when I was a young man sitting in jail, I told myself, *I'm done. It's over. I've thrown my life away. It's going to end a lot earlier than I ever expected, so I might as well go out strong.* Despite being surrounded by people who loved me—even a son and a wife—it didn't matter. Why? Because I wasn't in Christ. I was in Ed. And being in Ed is a bad place to be.

You don't want to be immersed in this world, living for this world, and thinking that this world is where your source of satisfaction will be. It will only bring condemnation. That's why, when you're in the flesh, condemnation messes with your head. You lose the sense of being in Christ.

Acting in the flesh doesn't change your status as a believer. However, it pulls you closer to the life you lived before you were saved. On top of that, you have the indwelling of the Holy Spirit in your life, who will not let you get away with anything. The Holy Spirit draws you and convicts you to bring you back to Christ. In Christ is the place of safety. You're secure in Him. It's a place of strength.

As Jesus put it, "This is the condemnation, that the light has come into the world, and men loved darkness rather than light, because their deeds were evil" (John 3:19). Jesus identifies where the condemnation lies. Condemnation is not in Christ. It's apart from Christ.

If you're reading this and you haven't been born again, today is the day. Now is the time! I don't know where you think your life is going to end, but the Bible says that apart from Christ, your life is going to end eternally separated from God. And that will be your just reward.

Make no mistake about it, God is fair and God is just. And He's the One who sacrificed His own Son to pay the penalty of your sin. He is a sinless God who meets you in your helpless state. Why? Because He loves you. And He's patient with you, so He might rescue you from yourself. Confess your sin, believe in Jesus' death and resurrection, and make Him the Lord of your life.

THE IMPORTANCE OF REMEMBERING THIS TRUTH

For those who are born again, condemnation can enter our lives because, over time, we forget. We forget the bondage that sin holds. It can be easy to walk away from God's faithfulness, even if it is only in our minds. Let's be encouraged by looking at a passage in Scripture.

In John 8, we meet a woman who was caught in the very act of her sin—*the very act*—a humiliating place to be. Let's look at what happens:

> Early in the morning He [Jesus] came again into the temple, and all the people came to Him; and He sat down and taught them. Then the scribes and Pharisees brought to Him a woman caught in adultery. And when they had set her in the midst, they said to Him, "Teacher, this woman was caught in adultery, in the very act" (John 8:2-4).

What was the act? The Bible speaks of it as adultery, which means she was having sex with a man who was not her husband. Then, the scribes and Pharisees told Jesus, "Now Moses, in the law, commanded us that such should be stoned" (verse 5). If they really believed what Moses said, they would have already killed this woman by heaving rocks at her. But they didn't do that. Why? Because they asked Jesus,

> "But what do You say?" This they said, testing Him, that they might have something of which to accuse Him (verse 6).

It is important to recognize that the woman was set up. She was used as a pawn. That's what religion does. It uses people. The religious rulers set her up. Even though there was a real sin that was part of her background, that was not the main thing. She was used, and that's always a sin. Abuse in any form in Jesus' church is a sin. It does not come from God. It's not God's will for any pastor, any lay leader, or anyone else in His church to perpetrate abuse of any kind on you, male or female, especially in the name of God.

Also, we read this passage in an environment far removed from the time and place in which it happened—often in a place that's clean and orderly. But the situation was not clean or orderly. It was messy. It was tumultuous and probably loud. The woman was disheveled. The passage doesn't even speak of her being covered up. But I hope she was.

The scribes and Pharisees brought the woman to Jesus, tears likely streaming. Their faces were fixed with anger. Not at her, she's just a pawn. They were abusing her. They wanted Jesus. They wanted to take Him out. So they brought this defenseless woman whom they had set up. Let's look at how Jesus responds:

> Jesus stooped down and wrote on the ground with His finger, as though He did not hear. So when they continued asking Him, He raised Himself up and said to them, "He who is without sin among you, let him throw a stone at her first." And again He stooped down and wrote on the ground. Then those who heard it, being convicted by their conscience, went out one by one, beginning with the oldest even to the last. And Jesus was left alone, and the woman standing in the midst (verses 6-9).

Although she was caught *in* the act, it took some time to bring her in front of Jesus. By the time her accusers dragged her into Jesus' presence, her act of adultery was in her past. She was no longer engaged in that sinful act. And Jesus' response highlights the reality that the scribes and the Pharisees also had past sin. Not only that, they were living in the present sin of using this woman to trap Jesus. The Bible tells us that we've all sinned and fallen short of the glory of God (Romans 3:23).

As Jesus was writing on the ground, the religious rulers weren't repentant. Their hearts weren't changing. Now, the woman wasn't receiving any attention from the crowd. Jesus was dealing with her accusers. Her accusers retreated.

Then, notice what Jesus said to her,

> "Woman, where are those accusers of yours? Has no one condemned you?" She said, "No one, Lord." And Jesus said to her, "Neither do I condemn you; go and sin no more" (John 8:10-11).

Pay attention to those ending words. If you battle condemnation, receive these words no matter the sin: "Neither do I condemn you." Circle, underline, or highlight them in your Bible. "Neither do I condemn you; go and sin no more." That's all that she needed.

I don't know why, but sometimes I argue with God. I can hear the voice of Jesus saying to me, *Neither do I condemn you, Ed; go and sin no more*. And yet, I condemn myself or allow others to condemn me about my past.

Perhaps some of you have found yourself in that same place. But we must remember, Jesus says, *Neither do I condemn you; go and sin no more. I forgive you. Past, present, and future, I forgive you.* In Christ, you're forgiven. And God's promise of forgiveness is all throughout the Bible.

- God spoke through Isaiah to tell us, "I, even I, am He who blots out your transgressions for My own sake; and I will not remember your sins" (Isaiah 43:25).
- Also through Isaiah, God said, "I have blotted out, like a thick cloud, your transgressions, and like a cloud, your sins. Return to Me, for I have redeemed you" (Isaiah 44:22).

- David said, "He has not dealt with us according to our sins, nor punished us according to our iniquities. For as the heavens are high above the earth, so great is His mercy toward those who fear Him" (Psalm 103:10-11).
- Peter said, "Repent therefore and be converted, that your sins may be blotted out, so that times of refreshing may come from the presence of the Lord" (Acts 3:19).
- And, as we've looked at closely, Paul said, "There is therefore now no condemnation to those who are in Christ" (Romans 8:1).

So answer this question for me: Are you in Christ? It's that simple. In Christ, there's no condemnation.

LIVING IN CHRIST APART FROM CONDEMNATION

As you move forward in your life in Christ, remember that you are no longer condemned by your past. You have the freedom to move away from your past and into your future. Here are a few practical tips to help you live your life in Christ apart from condemnation.

1. Don't confuse condemnation with conviction.

Condemnation and conviction are two very different things. Conviction of sin is a good thing. It's from God, and we need it. It's wholesome and valuable. The conviction of the Holy Spirit brings life and correction. On the other hand, condemnation brings death.

A simple way to remember this is: The conviction of sin draws you *to* God but condemnation leads you *away* from God. For example, often, people avoid going to church when they're under the weight of condemnation. When you're under the weight of condemnation, church is not an attractive place to be. You can misunderstand God and His heart toward you. You interpret it through glasses of condemnation. And when you put on glasses of condemnation, even the best encouragement is misinterpreted.

God wants to free you from sin. When Jesus ministered to the precious woman in John 8, He told her what she was doing was sin. He said, *Don't do it. Leave it behind you. Don't get caught up in this anymore. This life isn't good for you.* When everyone left and it was only Jesus and this woman under the weight of condemnation, He asked her, "Has no one condemned you?" Jesus did not condemn her either. But, He told her to go and *sin no more.*

Remember that the Holy Spirit will never condemn you. Never. The enemy of our soul—Satan—is the accuser of the brethren (Revelation 12:10), not God.

2. When you're convicted of sin, repent.

Did you know you can say you're sorry and never really mean it? True repentance will lead you away from sin. That's what repentance means.

The first step toward repentance is confession. That means you view your sin like God does. The Bible says, "If we confess our sins, He is faithful and just to forgive us our sins and to cleanse us from all unrighteousness" (1 John 1:9).

Confession and repentance—if you're struggling in this area, read Psalm 51. It's often referred to as the psalm of repentance. It was written by David who had much to repent from. David not only committed adultery, he had the woman's husband killed. Let the Holy Spirit use that psalm to do a work in your life. God will empower you, strengthen you, and help you.

3. Believe and act on God's Word.

I know it sounds simple. But when you hear truth, act on it. For example, in this chapter, you've learned about the life-giving message of Romans 8:1, "There is therefore now no condemnation for those who are in Christ." Believe what God says in that verse. Take the promise to heart. Trust that God means what He says—there's no condemnation for you in Christ.

You know where you stand right now. You might argue with me, saying, "But, Ed, it's not possible, not for me." But it's not about me. *God* says there's no condemnation for you. It's not about me or even about you. It's about Him. It's about the freedom God wants to give to you.

Jesus looks at you and asks, *Has anyone condemned you?* Unfortunately, you can't always answer no, like the woman did in John 8. But even when there are people who condemn you, remember, that is not coming from God. Jesus says to you, *I'm not condemning you. Go and sin no more.*

The simplicity of the Bible is life-giving. The Bible is alive and powerful. It's "sharper than any two-edged sword" (Hebrews 4:12). It makes sense that the enemy tries to keep you from it. Also, it makes sense that, when you're living in your flesh, you try to avoid it.

Have you ever noticed that distractions arise when you try to read the Bible? For example, if you use your phone to read it, a text message will pop up and interrupt your reading. You open the text message, and it takes you to Instagram. You scroll a little and before you know it, you've got to go to work. You tell yourself, *I'll read the Bible when I take a break at work.* But then, you get a phone call during your break. Then, it's lunchtime, and you can't find your phone. It all snowballs. The distractions can be endless.

Again, it makes sense. The enemy wants to separate you from the life-giving words of the Scriptures. Because if you don't hear the Word, you won't know the Word. And if you don't know the Word, you won't act on the Word.

Yet God has made our role easy for us. He doesn't require you to be a scholar, have a degree, or go to seminary. Simply read the Bible. God doesn't say you need to fully understand it. Just read it and apply it.

When you don't understand a passage or concept, it will drive you to God to ask Him what it means. You're going to win either way. Also, if you don't know what a word means, look it up. There are a lot of biblically sound resources you can look to for help. You can also lean on trusted believers to help you with your questions. Don't make excuses to not engage with God's Word.

As you learn what God's Word says, believe it and do it. Take the access God has given you. As the Bible says, in Romans 5:1-2,

> Having been justified by faith, we have peace with God through our Lord Jesus Christ, through whom also we have access by faith into this grace in which we stand, and rejoice in hope of the glory of God.

We have access by faith. Obey that word. Come in, and take the access that Jesus gives.

If you have doubt whether you are saved, believe what Jesus told us in John 5. He said, "Most assuredly, I say to you, he who hears My word and believes in Him who sent Me has everlasting life" (verse 24).

If you hear Jesus' Word and believe in the One who sent Him, you have everlasting life. You're saved. Don't give in to the doubt. Believe God's Word. God says, "If you confess with your mouth the Lord Jesus and believe in your heart that God has raised Him from the dead, you will be saved" (Romans 10:9). So live as a saved person.

Believers live by what God has said in the Bible because His Word is life. We don't live by our feelings. We don't live by our experiences.

It makes me think of Noah. Noah is recognized as a great example of faith in the "Hall of Faith" in Hebrews 11:7. Noah built an ark out of obedience, not understanding. Noah had no idea what a flood was. He simply heard God's Word, and he did it. The people around him mocked him and they made fun of him.

Who knows how Noah felt and what he thought? I wonder if he

felt silly, building a big boat when the world had never seen a drop of rain. I wonder if his wife pointed her finger at him and said, "You're crazy. Get that thing out of the front yard."

But Noah obeyed. He didn't build the ark because he felt like it. He built it because God commanded him to. Noah gives us an example to follow. He heard. He believed. And he acted. Doing those things will change your life.

4. Stop looking back.

No more looking back. Receive the word from Romans 8:1, "There is therefore now no condemnation to those who are in Christ." Memorize it. Believe it. Live it. A life of abiding in Christ does not lead to condemnation. It leads to victory and freedom and a remembrance of all that God has done on your behalf.

REFLECTION/DISCUSSION QUESTIONS

1. Which of the six signs of being prone to condemnation resonates the most with you?
2. Which of the truths in the Benefits of Being in Christ section do you struggle to believe? Why? Memorize and meditate on that truth this week and allow God to replace your thoughts and feelings with the truth.
3. What is something in your life that is not good for you, or you need to leave behind and stop getting caught up in?

3

DEALING WITH THE LAW OF GOD

In Romans 7, we read the confessions of an exhausted believer. Looking back on his life, the apostle Paul relived his own past—the wrestles and the struggles he went through. He wrote about how the law bound him tightly with all its rules and regulations. Paul had been bound and married to the law. The law was perfect, and it seemed to have no escape.

But there was an escape. The escape was not physical; it was spiritual death. When, by faith, he became bound to Jesus Christ—the One who fulfilled the law—he was released from the expectations, demands, and perfections of the law.

You too are released from the law when you place your faith in Jesus Christ, die to yourself, and live unto Christ. The way to be free from the demands of the law is to live a new life in Christ. In Christ, you are a new creation, "old things have passed away; behold, all things have become new" (2 Corinthians 5:17).

THE BATTLE BETWEEN THE SPIRIT AND THE FLESH

Yet in freedom from the law and the newness of life in Jesus, there remains a problem. All of us who live by faith in Jesus still retain our flesh—the carnality of our minds and the legality of our humanity.

In the Bible, when the word *flesh* is used in a spiritual context, it's not in reference to the skin on your bones. It's not making a statement about the physical. Instead, it means to live according to your own resources. It's literally the opposite of Proverbs 3:5, which tells us to "trust in the Lord with all your heart, and lean not on your own understanding."

When you lean on your own understanding, you're in the flesh. You're relying on your own resources. As smart as you may be and as smart as you might become, you will never be as smart as God. And your resources and abilities pale in comparison to God's power. What man is unable to do, God is able to do.

There is a battle between the flesh and the Spirit. Everything is tainted by sin. Even on our best days, we're imperfect. The best that we can offer God on our own is flawed and soiled by sin.

When you hear the phrase *battling the flesh*, think of it as a battle against your old sinful habit patterns. Let's say you're in the garage, hammering a nail into a piece of wood and with an errant swing you hit your thumb really hard. Your first response will give you a good idea of the state of your flesh.

Many of us will blurt out something that you haven't heard come out of your mouth in 20 years. Why? Because you're in the flesh. It was a bad habit to say those words back then (and remains so now). But those patterns still exist in your life. The same holds true even if the words don't come out of your mouth. Maybe instead, you only think them in your head. But the words still come to mind, even if you don't say them out loud.

When the Bible says that you're a new creation in Christ, it speaks of your spiritual life, which is being renewed day by day. Your brain is still the same old brain in your head. But God is renewing your mind. You're growing in grace. You still wage a battle with your flesh.

For those of us who got saved later in life, we have sinful habits that are deep-seated. We may not be living in those sinful habits anymore. Praise God for that! That should no longer be the manner of your life. But because they were a part of your past, they become a point of battle against your flesh. As the Bible tells us, "The flesh lusts against the Spirit, and the Spirit against the flesh; and these are contrary to one another, so that you do not do the things that you wish" (Galatians 5:17).

The word *lust* means a strong craving. Often, we use the term when we're talking about sexual sin. In that context, it means someone experiences a strong craving for sexual sin. However, the word can be used to describe a strong craving for a lot of other things as well.

When the Bible says the flesh lusts against the Spirit, it means there's a battle over what you will yield to in your life. Will you yield to the indwelling power of God in you—the Holy Spirit—who wants to lead you in paths of righteousness and purity, ultimately pleasing God? Or will you yield to your own sinful habits?

But responding to the Spirit is not easy. It is much easier for us to place ourselves back under the law. Rules and regulations can feel like a place of safety. For instance, you might decide,

> *I've had a bad day. Starting tomorrow, I'm going to get up at 7:00 am, open my Bible, write a journal entry, and do my devotional time for exactly 15 minutes. Then, the next day, I'll do 20 minutes. The next day, 25 minutes. And on Sunday, I'm going to get up extra early. Not only am I going to do my devotional time, I'm going to go to church as well. And I might even stay at church after the service ends.*

So you begin this new routine. Your rules are meaningful to you. They're attainable. And when you follow through on them, you feel good. The days you wake up at 7:00 am and do your devos, you think to yourself, *Ah, that felt good. I'm so right with God.*

But then, you have a bad day. You don't get up at 7:00 am. In setting up a law for yourself and failing to keep it, the law condemns you and accuses you. And what's worse, it uses your voice to do so. You think to yourself, *I didn't get up at 7:00 am! I must be a horrible Christian.*

And it tends to pile on throughout the day. You make a mistake in the afternoon—you get mad at your kids. And you think, *I'm a horrible parent.* Or you mess up at work and tell yourself, *I'm a horrible employee.*

Why are you doing this? Because you didn't keep your own rules. You set up a system that took you away from the grace of God—away from enjoying Him—through both the good and the bad. I hope you know that even if you wake up at 7:05 am and forget your devotional time, God still loves you. He still cares for you.

That's what Paul was wrestling with in Romans 7. There was a season in Paul's life when he went back under the law, underneath its rules and regulations. And he gave us insight into what it feels like. This might be present in your life. Paul said,

> We know that the law is spiritual, but I am carnal, sold under sin. For what I am doing, I do not understand. For what I will to do, that I do not practice; but what I hate, that I do. If, then, I do what I will not to do, I agree with the law that it is good. But now, it is no longer I who do it, but sin that dwells in me. For I know that in me (that is, in my flesh) nothing good dwells (Romans 7:14-18).

Nothing good dwells in us. The good in your life comes from your relationship with Jesus Christ. And He's making you better every day. Jesus is developing you and pouring more of Himself into you as you yield your life to Him.

THE LAW CANNOT CHANGE YOU

Paul knew that nothing good dwelt in him. He recognized that he couldn't change himself. And he knew that the law couldn't change him either. Paul continued,

> For to will is present with me, but how to perform what is good I do not find. For the good that I will to do, I do not do; but the evil I will not to do, that I practice. Now if I do what I will not to do, it is no longer I who do it, but sin that dwells in me.
>
> I find then a law, that evil is present with me, the one who wills to do good. For I delight in the law of God according to the inward man. But I see another law in my members, warring against the law of my mind, and bringing me into captivity to the law of sin which is in my members. O wretched man that I am! Who will deliver me from this body of death? I thank God—through Jesus Christ our Lord!
>
> So then, with the mind I myself serve the law of God, but with the flesh the law of sin.
>
> There is therefore now no condemnation to those who are in Christ Jesus, who do not walk according to the flesh, but according to the Spirit. For the law of the Spirit of life in Christ Jesus has made me free from the law of sin and death. For what the law could not do in that it was weak through the flesh, God did by sending His own Son in the likeness of sinful flesh, on account of sin: He condemned sin in the flesh, that the righteous requirement of the law might be fulfilled in us who do not walk according to the flesh but according to the Spirit. For those who live

> according to the flesh set their minds on the things of the flesh, but those who live according to the Spirit, the things of the Spirit. For to be carnally minded is death, but to be spiritually minded is life and peace (Romans 7:18–8:6).

What the law couldn't do, God did. How? By sending Jesus Christ. What was the law unable to do? The law was unable to change us. Like a mirror does not possess any power to change what it reveals, the law has no power to change a person. It simply reveals.

Laws don't impress upon people who are not breaking the law. It's only when you break the law that the law singles you out and says, "You're a lawbreaker." The law has your attention. Like when a police officer (think back to chapter 2), clocks you driving 35 miles per hour in a 25-mile-per-hour zone. He pulls you over and points out the black-and-white sign that reads: Speed 25. Even if you didn't see the sign, the law speaks. And it condemns you.

If you were driving 25 miles per hour, the law wouldn't condemn you because you're not a lawbreaker. When you compare the sign to your speedometer and they match, there's comfort. There's no battle. But it is when your speedometer exceeds the posted limit, there's a great battle.

For those of you who broke the laws of man quite a bit before you were saved, you likely remember how frequently you would look over your shoulder. And for those who didn't, you can still likely relate through former trespasses at work, school, or in your home because you would find yourself doing the same thing, albeit with different consequences. When we violate the rules, we find ourselves on edge, constantly peeking around the corner and checking things out. However, when we aren't in violation of the rules or laws, we find ourselves at ease.

We can feel the same way when it comes to the things of God. When you're walking in the Spirit, the Bible is alive to you. Your life matches God's law, and you enjoy it. But when you start sinfully speeding through life, you become uncomfortable with God's law.

For example, suppose you get upset with someone and do not treat them with kindness. When you're reminded that the Bible says, "Be kind to one another" (Ephesians 4:32), you get mad at the Bible. Or you make an excuse for why you didn't need to be kind. You tell yourself that the person deserved the treatment you gave them. These responses come from the flesh and are destructive. When you do this, you're positioning yourself in the place of God and writing your own law that is not found in the Bible.

Paul was struggling. He was wrestling. He described what we very much feel at times. *The things I want to do, I don't do. And the things I don't want to do, I do. What is going on?* The flesh. That's what's going on.

Reading through Romans 7 can be exhausting. We recognize ourselves in Paul's struggle. You find yourself asking the questions: *What am I doing? What has happened to me? What kind of Christian life is this? What does it mean to follow Jesus?* Then, you plead: *I'm trying. I'm trying.*

Recently, someone mentioned to me, "I'm trying." My automatic response was, "No, there's no such thing as trying. Do it!" Trying is not doing. Trying is not yielding and abiding. It gets frustrating. It's a battle. You find yourself wondering, *Who's going to deliver me from this?* But in the midst of the struggle, remember what Paul shared. It is exhausting because you can't win the battle using your own strength. You can't will yourself to victory. You can't read enough self-help books or complete enough Bible studies. You can't do it. It's impossible.

Why? It's impossible because God's standard is perfection. And no one is perfect—you're not perfect and neither am I.

JESUS DELIVERS US FROM THE LAW

The key to the struggle is not *how* you get out of it, but instead, *Who* will deliver you from it. When you focus on the how, that's the law.

However, when you focus on the Who, you can see the grace. And there is a big difference.

Too many Christians spend their lives asking, "How?" "How do I get over this struggle?" "How do I get through that trial?" "How?" But the real issue in your life isn't how, it's Who. Who will deliver you from this body of death? Who will come to your rescue? If you live your Christian life clinging to the *how* questions, you'll be spiritually exhausted. You'll be that wretched man (Romans 7:24).

Now, I understand there is a place that allows for instruction. The Bible speaks of discipleship. A regular part of Jesus' ministry was spent teaching. That's not what I'm referring to. When I am talking about living by asking the how questions, I'm referring to those who are looking for a quick fix, people who are only looking for the steps they need to follow.

If you came to me with a problem and I gave you a list of the steps you should take to solve the problem, you would be relieved. You'd think you had the solution in your hands. But your respite comes for the wrong reasons. Your relief wouldn't be based on your trust and faith in Jesus. It would be based on my experience as a Bible teacher. And that peace and comfort would only be temporary.

As you work through the list, you will fail. That's the problem with lists, rules, and regulations. Your desire to have a manual ultimately will not help you. Only God can do a transformative work in you. It's the newness of the Spirit—Christ in you—not the letter of the law that brings life. That's the new covenant.

Who will deliver you? Christ in you, the hope of glory. Day by day, He is working in you. As Paul said, "I thank God—through Jesus Christ our Lord!" (verse 25). Jesus is our deliverer. He lives in us and helps us from the inside. He strengthens us. He encourages us. He helps us to believe the promises of God!

That is something that I could never do for you. As a man of God—a fellow brother, pastor, and servant—I can never help you from the inside. Never. That's not the realm that God has given to me. I can't help you from the inside. I can only point you to the One who can. I can only remind you of His presence. I can only help you see His strength.

A PICTURE OF GRACE IN THE LIFE OF NOAH

Grace doesn't appear for the first time in the New Testament. From the very beginning of creation, God demonstrated His grace to us. God is a God of grace. The grace of God—the scarlet thread of God's redemption through Jesus Christ—is all throughout the Bible. Let's dive deeper into the story of Noah to see a picture of it. It's very encouraging.

In Genesis 5:29, the Bible introduces us to a special man named Noah. We learn that "Noah found grace in the eyes of the Lord" (6:8). The earth had become corrupt and filled with violence, and God had decided to destroy it. But God also established a covenant with Noah to preserve him and his family. Noah was given very specific instructions about how to build an ark. Within those instructions, we are given a picture of God's grace. God told Noah, "Make yourself an ark of gopherwood; make rooms in the ark, and cover it inside and outside with pitch" (verse 14). God told Noah to use pitch. The Hebrew word for pitch is *koper*.[1] This word is derived from the Hebrew root word *kapar*,[2] which means "atonement."

Atonement is a technical word that means forgiveness. It speaks of God's mercy in forgiving our sins. A way that you can remember this meaning is to break down the word into three parts: at-one-ment. *Atonement* means that you and I are made one with God. We're brought into unity with God because our sins have been forgiven, and the wrath of God is no longer upon us.

Noah was told to build a wooden ark and he was to cover it with pitch. The ark becomes a type for the atonement of Jesus Christ. It's a picture of Jesus. The only way Noah and his family could be saved was to be *inside* the ark. That was God's instruction—for Noah and his family to go into the ark (Genesis 7:1).

The Bible tells us that the Lord shut the door of the ark (Genesis 7:16). Noah's family didn't need to engineer a system for sealing themselves inside. God shut them in. And for 40 days and 40 nights, the rain came down and the waters—the judgment of God—began to rise. But Noah and his family remained in the ark—covered, protected, and safe.

Today, aren't you glad that God told Noah and his family to go inside the ark, and sealed it behind them? Imagine if God had said,

> *Noah, the storms are coming, the floods are coming, and the destruction is coming. Here's what I want you to do: Build an ark and put handles on the inside of the door. To keep the door closed for 40 days and 40 nights, you and your family will need to hang on for dear life. If you hang on to the end, you'll be safe.*

God didn't say that! The family's survival wasn't dependent on Noah's ability to hold on to a handle in order to be saved from judgment. Likewise, it wasn't about his family's abilities either. You can sort of picture them holding on for a couple of hours, or maybe a little longer. But they wouldn't have made it 40 days. Thankfully, God didn't tell them to hold on for dear life. He had them go into the ark. And then, He shut them inside where they would be safe.

How was Noah preserved from the judgment of God through the flood? He was preserved in the same way you and I are preserved—by grace, through faith. It was a "gift of God, not of works, lest anyone should boast" (Ephesians 2:8-9). Noah is a great example. He found grace in the eyes of God. The grace of God saved Noah and his family from destruction.

God doesn't ask you or me to hold on for dear life either. No, He tells us, *Get inside, I'll shut you in. Do you want to let go of your past? Get inside.* The safest place for you to be is hidden in Christ. The Bible says, in Colossians 3:3, "You died, and your life is hidden with Christ in God." You're hidden.

In an effort to stay away from sin, many Christians desperately try to hold on to handles inside the door of the ark. You may not realize it, but you hear indicators of this all the time. For example, when you ask someone, "How are you doing today?" Many reply, "Hanging in there." You could stump them by replying, "Really, so you're hanging on to the handles inside the ark?"

Just hanging in there—that's a reflection that someone is about to give in. When you use that vernacular—whether you mean it in a spiritual way or not—it's not actually about you hanging in there. It's about God's firm grip on your life. Even if you let go, God is holding on to you. The Bible tells us, a righteous man may fall seven times, but he'll rise again (Proverbs 24:16). That is the faithfulness of God.

As we learned from Romans 8:1, there is therefore now no condemnation in Christ. That's where freedom from your past comes—to be in Christ and the newness of His work. When the Father looks at you and me, He doesn't see all our failures and faults. Although He knows everything about us, He chooses to see us in Christ. Not only does Jesus come to live in you, but you're also put in Him. You're covered both ways. You are sealed.

GRACE SUPERSEDES THE LAW OF SIN AND DEATH

We have great freedom in Christ. According to Romans 8:2, "The law of the Spirit of life in Christ Jesus has made [us] free from the law of sin and death." What is the Spirit of life in Christ? It's the gospel. The good news is the freedom of the Spirit of life.

You see, the law wasn't done away with. The law shows us our need for Jesus. It's still doing its job. It's holy. It's just. And it's good. As we learn from Galatians 3:24, "The law was our tutor to bring us to Christ, that we might be justified by faith."

The law can refer to a few things. It could be a reference to the Ten Commandments, the first five books of the Old Testament known as the Torah, or the Mosaic Covenant. It's the reality of God's demands upon our lives, given in His teachings and instructions to the Jewish people, revealing His desire for their (and our) purity. And the law instructs us repeatedly that each one of us is a sinner and must surely die. That's the root of the law.

The law of sin and death is like the force of gravity. When you walk through a terminal at an airport, out the windows you see plane after plane parked at their gates. Why? Because gravity is acting on each one. But there will come a time when those same planes will be in flight. When a pilot starts up the engines and guides the plane down the runway, other laws of aerodynamics take over. New forces, thrust and lift, supersede weight (gravity) and drag. Does that mean that the force of gravity goes away? No. It still does its job. And it works perfectly without being changed. Other forces simply have a greater effect on the aircraft.

So too with the law of sin and death. Grace supersedes that law. In Christ, you're no longer bound to the old law. In Christ, you're under the law of the Spirit of life. Jesus set us free from the law of sin and death. We are free to live for Jesus by faith.

There were people who went to Jesus and asked Him, "What shall we do, that we may work the works of God?" (John 6:28). That's a common question people still ask today. People want something they can do. We're tethered to the law, motivated by it, striving to attain it, and working hard to please God. But pay careful attention to Jesus' answer. He said, "This is the work of God, that you believe in Him whom He sent" (verse 29).

We are free—not by working hard or doing more; not by following rules and regulations; and certainly not by dressing well, using the right language, having perfect devotional times, or reading through the Bible a million times. It comes by faith. We are made free by faith. The Spirit of life that lives in you draws you away from the law of sin and death. You're not bound by it any longer.

I love what we are told in Romans 8:3: "What the law could not do in that it was weak through the flesh, God did by sending His own Son." The law cannot give life. It cannot give power. The law has no ability to forgive. Forgiveness only comes from God through Jesus Christ. What the law couldn't do, God did. How? By sending Jesus Christ to die for you and me.

Living by God's grace sets you free from the past. It gives you true freedom. The law is weak because it cannot change your flesh. Your inability to keep the law reveals its weakness. The law can't change you from the inside out. You can't follow enough rules and lists, and you can't read enough books to make you right with God.

If you're still not convinced, write down your goals on index cards and post them all over your house. The only thing you'll consistently recognize when you see those cards is your weakness because of your inability to perfectly follow through with your goals. If you possessed the strength to follow through with them, you wouldn't need a reminder on an index card.

Reminders are good, that's not the issue. But every time we need to be reminded, all it does is reveal our weakness. Our inability to execute on everything shows our weakness, not our strength.

For instance, even if you write one simple message on multiple cards: *I will be a good person today, the best person I could ever be*, and you put a card on the mirror, one on your shoe, one in your car, and you memorize this message, you've placed a heavy burden on yourself. Of course, it's good to be good. But every day, with that little goal, you'll need to be better than you were the day before, or you've failed. If Monday was your best day, then when you wake up in the morning on Tuesday, you're going to have to be even better than you were on Monday. Or maybe, you set the bar on being good so low that you can always hit it. However, you will feel guilty because you know that each day your effort wasn't your best. Striving to be better each day on our own will always end up coming up short.

Another thing we do is set up rules and regulations that we believe we can follow, but others can't. Let me illustrate it this way: Have you noticed that your own sin looks bad when it is present in someone else's life? You seem to notice certain sins in other people's lives. You are shocked by them, and you may even say, "I can't believe they did that." But, over time, God reveals that the sin you've been noticing in others' lives is a reminder of the sin that you need to deal with in your own life.

There's an example of this in the Bible. The Lord sent Nathan to his friend King David, and Nathan told David a story:

> There were two men in one city, one rich and the other poor. The rich man had exceedingly many flocks and herds. But the poor man had nothing, except one little ewe lamb which he had bought and nourished; and it grew up together with him and with his children. It ate of his own food and drank from his own cup and lay in his bosom; and it was like a daughter to him. And a traveler came to the rich man, who refused to take from his own flock and from his own herd to prepare one for the wayfaring man who had come to him; but he took the poor man's lamb and prepared it for the man who had come to him (2 Samuel 12:1-4).

It was a great injustice, and David got angry. What was the first consequence that David pronounced against the rich man in that story? Death. David said, "As the LORD lives, the man who has done this shall surely die!" (verse 5).

The death penalty wasn't even appropriate for the crime. The punishment should have been for the rich man to give two lambs to the poor man. But what was on David's mind? The death penalty. Why? Because he was a murderer. David had committed adultery, and then, he had the woman's husband killed in battle to cover up his sin (2 Samuel 11). We *all* sin.

The law doesn't bring you freedom. Only Jesus Christ can do that. God did what the law couldn't do. He sent His own Son to die for you. And by placing your faith in Jesus, freedom is yours. By faith in Him, you fulfill all the requirements of the law.

If you want to let go of your past, you need to be in Christ. Jesus does the work. He empowers, helps, and strengthens you. He is faithful to give you the power to fulfill everything that He asks you to do.

As the Bible instructs,

> We have such trust through Christ toward God. Not that we are sufficient of ourselves to think of anything as being from ourselves, but our sufficiency is from God (2 Corinthians 3:4-5).

That is the language of grace. We have nothing to offer. Our sufficiency is in Christ. It comes from God.

> [God] made us sufficient as ministers of the new covenant, not of the letter but of the Spirit; for the letter kills, but the Spirit gives life.
>
> But if the ministry of death, written and engraved on stones, was glorious, so that the children of Israel could not look steadily at the face of Moses because of the glory of his countenance, which glory was passing away, how

> will the ministry of the Spirit not be more glorious? For if the ministry of condemnation had glory, the ministry of righteousness exceeds much more in glory. For even what was made glorious had no glory in this respect, because of the glory that excels. For if what is passing away was glorious, what remains is much more glorious (2 Corinthians 3:6-11).

Let's look at the contrast:

- The Old Covenant is the law of sin and death. The New Covenant is the law of the Spirit of life.
- The Old Covenant is the ministry of death. But the New Covenant is the ministry of life.
- The Old Covenant was written on stones. It was external. It was demanding. It required outward change in conformity to a list. But the New Covenant is written on hearts, as promised in Jeremiah 31:33 and Ezekiel 36:26.

God promised to do a work in the hearts of men. God gives us a new nature. It's an internal change that causes you to desire to do the will of God. You are not to desire following a list of commands.

For example, many Christians will emphasize and assert that the way you dress can make you more spiritual. The Bible teaches on modesty for both men and women. But creating a theology of dress to a level of detail that is outside of the Bible's instruction is adding an external list of rules to what really matters, the gospel.

External effort is not what God is looking for. He desires to see the internal work of His Spirit. The Old Covenant was temporary. Its glory faded away. But the New Covenant is eternal in glory and righteousness. The Old Covenant was condemnation. But the New Covenant gives justification and the forgiveness of sins.

How are we able to let go of our past? Through God's Spirit who dwells in us. Any inability to be free from our past reflects our own human effort. When you attempt to address sin on your own, you subject yourself to the law of sin and death. But when you choose to obey God—when you release yourself to the law of the Spirit of life—you are instantly free.

Now you may return to old patterns. You may try to order your life as if the law of sin and death still holds power in the life of the believer. However, you can live in freedom again when you choose to believe what God has promised in Romans 8. Don't go back to being the person described by Paul in Romans 7. When you read through the book of Romans, you'll notice a progression of victory and joy.

I pray you recognize that God is the One who will set you free. It's not done by your own effort. When we try to live by our own effort, we make things worse, not better. And we delay the enjoyment of the very presence of God in our lives.

Instead, freedom is brought on by faith, trusting in God's power. Believe that God did what He has said He has done. And trust that God will continue to do what He has said He will do. Freedom will come as you surrender your life to Him.

REFLECTION/DISCUSSION QUESTIONS

1. What is something that you are still struggling with (trying your hardest to hold on to the handles) that the Lord is asking you to surrender?

2. Remember a time or situation when all you wanted to do was to get out of the trial you were experiencing, but now looking back, you can see the Lord was working. What did He show you?

3. Are you prone to making lists of Christian dos and don'ts that are keeping you from seeing the grace God has for you? What is an area of your life where you are simply going through the motions and you need to return to your "first love" (Revelation 2:4) and do so wholeheartedly?

4

DEALING WITH YOUR PAST

Everyone has a past—a past that's been touched by sin. People have hurt you. And you've likely done things you regret. What comes to mind when you think about your past? Are there experiences you wish weren't a part of your testimony? Are there events that you wish would disappear or that you could wipe clean?

This is where Romans 8:1 enters our lives. Because no matter what comes to mind, "there is therefore now no condemnation for those who are in Christ Jesus"—your past included. You are not declared guilty because of your past, you are saved from it.

However, in living with the reality of your past, a question remains. And it is a good question. What is to be done with your past? Graciously, the Bible provides the answers. There are three tasks to commit to: forget, forgive, and forsake.

FORGETTING YOUR PAST

First, you forget your past. As Paul told us,

> Not that I have already attained, or am already perfected; but I press on, that I may lay hold of that for which Christ

> Jesus has also laid hold of me. Brethren, I do not count myself to have apprehended; but one thing I do, *forgetting* those things which are behind and reaching forward to those things which are ahead, I press toward the goal for the prize of the upward call of God in Christ Jesus (Philippians 3:12-14, emphasis added).

Forgetting those things that are behind you, press forward. Now, I know this sounds too simple. But it's only simplistic if you approach it that way. You are not trying to erase a memory. Instead, you are making a conscious choice to move forward. We forget the past by releasing the past and reaching for the future.

You cannot reach forward if you're still holding on to the past. You won't make progress if you choose to look backward.

When you drive your car, have you ever thought about how big your windshield is? It's huge compared to your rearview mirror. Do you usually drive in reverse all the way to your destination by looking in your little rearview mirror? Or do car manufacturers make cars that have a windshield that is the size of a rearview mirror? Of course not. Because the best way to drive a car is by driving it forward.

You won't get very far if you're always looking in your rearview mirror. It's only a matter of time before you'll crash and hurt yourself and others.

Don't look backward. Make a conscious choice to forget the past and remember that God has forgiven you. Over time, your past is going to come up. You're going to bring it up. Others will bring it up. Memories will come into your mind. And each time this happens, regardless of the cause, you need to decide to forget it. Choose not to dwell in the past anymore.

I have found that the only time I fail to forget my past is when I choose to dwell on it. Can you relate to that? When I dwell on the past, I'm choosing to remember it. I make a conscious decision to hang out there and think about it for a while. You know how it goes, you begin to think about it, and then, you start to drown in the sorrow and grief that it brings you. You forget all that God has done. And before you know it, you're finished.

Choose to forget the past. Don't dwell on it. Yes, it was painful. Yes, you were hurt. But it's in the past. It's over. It's done.

In Philippians 3:12-14, Paul urges us to forget those things in the past, and press on. Press toward the goal. The phrase *press on* means "to run swiftly."[1] It paints a picture of moving quickly and going after it. That's what Paul did. He ran swiftly away from his past and swiftly toward the goal of Jesus Christ.

You must forget the past. Although you may think that you can't, in Christ, you can.

When I share my testimony, I do so not as an anchor holding me back in my life, but in light of the reality of what God has delivered me from. Today, my past has perspective. I'm not proud of my past. Nor do I choose to dwell on it. But if God can use the delivering power that He's demonstrated in my life, I will continue to share my testimony for the sake of deliverance in others' lives.

I can't help but think that someone reading this is in great bondage. When you're in great bondage, you don't believe that you'll be delivered. You can't envision the possibility of it. You don't even have a concept of how life could be different—until someone else comes along and shows you.

That's what happened to me. I remember it distinctly. I was listening to the testimony of pastor Raul Ries. I can still remember where I was sitting and the sound of his voice. And I remember the freedom that was spoken into my life through the Word of God and through a man who was a sinner like me. Raul's testimony was where my future was headed if God didn't intervene. As I listened to him, I thought, *Man, if God can change this guy, then maybe…*

At the time, I didn't fully believe it. But that thought put me on the path of considering that God could do that in my life. And it gave me hope.

Surprisingly, the worst counselor in your life is not a friend. Nor is it a person who may give you bad advice. Often, the worst counselor in your life tends to be you.

Did you know that you talk to yourself more than you do to anyone else? And that's not a weird thing. We all reason with ourselves and think through our circumstances. We have discussions with ourselves that are in no way unhealthy. It occurs daily, multiple times per day, to every one of us.

But when we enter that mode, we must make a choice. Either we will counsel ourselves with the Word of God and His truths, or we will counsel ourselves with our own understanding. And we make great mistakes when we talk to ourselves without the Word of God open or the Word of God speaking to us.

You must forget the past. I've found that the only time I can forget my past is when I choose to dwell on my future. I can't think about two things at the same time. When I'm meditating on the Scriptures day and night, like God told Joshua to do (Joshua 1:8), I find myself enraptured in the potential of what God wants to do in my life. But if I dwell on some of my current circumstances, or something that happened yesterday, last week, or five and a half years ago, then I'm sunk.

Have you ever been there? Depression, discouragement, sorrow, and feeling sorry for yourself are always only one decision away. And those things are not from the Lord. They come from a weight of condemnation; a choice to reject God's will for your life. When you choose to repeatedly play your past over in your mind, it will bury you.

It's tempting to relive your past. Maybe you had an argument with someone. You replay that argument and think of all the things you said or could have said. You think, *Oh man, I could've said that instead.* But you can't say those things now. It's over.

The reality is that those who choose not to forget tend to remain in one place their whole lives. A place of hurt or failure. That's where they're stuck. When you talk to them, that's what they talk about. Everyone around them has moved on, but they've chosen not to move forward.

If that's you, I encourage you to stop living in the past. Don't misunderstand me. I realize that things happen in life that are extremely painful. I know some of you have been violated and greatly hurt. Some of you have done great damage to your minds and your bodies. But Jesus is cleansing, washing, and changing you. He's redeemed you. And whatever has happened is over. You're not there anymore.

When we are in Christ, there's no condemnation for us or for others. But the enemy's trap has been set. And it's always ready to take you back, if you allow it to.

I know some of you reading this are wrestling with me. You're battling this concept, this truth of forgetting and moving forward. You may be arguing with me. And you might even be thinking, *Ed, you just don't understand. If you were to walk in my shoes for a week, you would understand.*

Well, I must admit that I don't *fully* understand your personal pain, problems, or thoughts. I don't. There's no need to argue with me over that point. I don't understand every problem in everyone's life. But that's really good news—our freedom doesn't depend on our own understanding.

I believe I possess a deeper empathy these days than in years past—a deeper compassion for people's pain and problems. But my empathy will only help you to get to Jesus Christ. See, it's not whether I understand your circumstances or not. If I were in your shoes, I'd probably hurt the way you hurt. And I'd probably face the same temptations you're facing. I'd be sitting in your seat. The answer for all of us is the same. Jesus Christ has come to forgive us of all our sins, so we can forgive others and be free. He has forgiven us, so we can live a life that honors and pleases Him. It's okay if you argue with me on this point, but I will tell you it's a waste of time. We often get defensive when the truth starts to get close. Defensiveness is always a sign that something's touched you. It's self-protection.

But aren't you tired of needing to protect yourself and repeatedly dealing with the same issues? Do you yearn and hope for a better day? A better week? A better month? It's available to you now, in Christ.

In a believer's life, the root of condemnation is always tied to looking back. After all, what would the enemy condemn you for regarding your future? You don't know what the future holds. It hasn't been lived out. The root of condemnation is always in the past. You can't be condemned when you're looking upward and forward. That's why the enemy loves for you to look back on the past and keep your eyes focused on sin—your sin or someone else's that affected you. The enemy knows that if he can get people to look back on their past, many of them will remain there.

For that reason, I've made a practice of being guarded. I am deliberately careful when sharing about my past—even about what I share with you in this book. I don't want to go back to the past. And I don't want to stay there. I must say, many of the regrets in my life were a product of the "old Ed." And the good news is that the Bible says the old Ed is dead. That's the truth. I'm a new creation in Christ (2 Corinthians 5:17). In Christ, the "old you" is dead as well. You are a new creation!

For those of you who struggle with forgetting your past, let me ask you: Are you actively choosing to stay in your past, to dwell on it? Do you want to be one of the many people who live in the past, stay there, and never discover their future or truly enjoy the presence of the Lord?

Your future is literally moments away. It's only one decision away. Let go of your past. God is telling you to let go. He's telling you to move on. Because you are free in Christ.

FORGIVING YOUR PAST

Second, in dealing with your past, you need to forgive it. Forgiveness is the key to a healthy, vibrant life in Christ.

There are lessons we can learn from Jesus in a story found in Luke 15. It's a familiar story for some.

> A certain man had two sons. And the younger of them said to his father, "Father, give me the portion of goods that falls to me." So [the father] divided to them his livelihood (Luke 15:11-12).

What did the son do exactly? By asking for his inheritance early, the son, in effect, said to his father, "I wish you were dead. I don't want the kind of relationship that we have today. I want what is mine. When you die, I get a portion of your wealth. But I want that portion now."

The son was truly separated from his dad at the point that he decided to communicate his demand. His heart was full of selfishness. And his father granted the request. Let's look at what the son did with his inheritance:

> Not many days after, the younger son gathered all together, journeyed to a far country, and there wasted his possessions with prodigal living (verse 13).

The son chose to live a sinful life. He left Israel. He left the comfort of his home and his family. He literally left his senses.

Look at the verbs used in verse 13, "the younger son gathered… journeyed…wasted…" That's what sin will do to you. It takes you to a place where you don't want to be. It will waste you. In other words, you will be ruined.

Right now, you may be facing a decision in your life that will take you down one of two opposite paths. One path requires a holy choice that you could make unto the Lord. The other path requires a little compromise. If you choose the path of compromise, as you gather and journey, you're going to waste at least a portion of your life. You may waste a day or two, a month, or a couple of years. But it will be a waste.

That's what the son did. He squandered everything. He took all that his dad had given to him and wasted it.

> When he had spent all, there arose a severe famine in that land, and he began to be in want. Then he went and joined himself to a citizen of that country, and he sent him into his fields to feed swine. And he would gladly have filled his stomach with the pods that the swine ate, and no one gave him anything (verses 14-16).

The son began to be in want. The world will never satisfy you. Have you noticed that in your own life? The son was better off in the time before he claimed his inheritance. And then, the son was in need. He was so hungry that he was willing to eat the pigs' food.

In that moment, the son finally came to his senses.

> When he came to himself, he said, "How many of my father's hired servants have bread enough and to spare, and I perish with hunger! I will arise and go to my father, and will say to him, 'Father, I have sinned against heaven and before you, and I am no longer worthy to be called your son. Make me like one of your hired servants'" (verses 17-19).

It says that "he came to himself." When he did, he returned home to his father.

Some of you may be praying for prodigal sons and daughters in your lives today. You need to pray that they will come to the end of themselves. It might be a prayer like, *Whatever it takes, Lord. Help them to recognize and realize that where they're at now is not Your best for them. Whatever it takes, bring them home.* And if you yourself have already taken a path of compromise, you can repent and turn from it right now. Don't waste any more time.

> He arose and came to his father. But when he was still a great way off, his father saw him and had compassion, and ran and fell on his neck and kissed him. And the son said to him, "Father, I have sinned against heaven and in your sight, and am no longer worthy to be called your son" (verses 20-21).

I know we call this story the parable of the prodigal son. But if you took a pen and circled every time the word father is mentioned, I think you would agree with me that it's truly the parable of the loving father.

The father ran toward his repentant son and received him. He didn't wait for the son to come all the way back home. He is the kind of father who would have gazed down the road every single day since his son left, longing to see his beloved son again. And the moment he saw his son, he ran to him. The father had already forgiven the wandering son. He was ready to forgive before the two even had a chance to talk. He didn't wait for an explanation. He welcomed his son as soon as he had come home.

Isn't that a great picture of our heavenly Father? When you turn back to Jesus, that's what the Father does in your life. He runs to you. He doesn't wait for you to come all the way. He does not stand there with His arms crossed in anger. Our God is full of love, mercy, and compassion. When you turn back after days, months, or years of prodigal living, He runs to you with forgiveness.

However, we read that the son still condemns himself. He says,

"Father, I have sinned against heaven and in your sight, and am no longer worthy to be called your son" (verse 21). The son felt unworthy. He was under a cloud of self-condemnation.

But look at what the father did. The father told his servants:

> "Bring out the best robe and put it on him, and put a ring on his hand and sandals on his feet. And bring the fatted calf here and kill it, and let us eat and be merry; for this my son was dead and is alive again; he was lost and is found." And they began to be merry (verses 22-24).

That sounds like a great end to the story, right? Everything's wonderful. The prodigal son came back, and he repented. He has learned. He has changed. He is washed and cleansed. He is not a servant; he's a son. And he receives forgiveness from his father.

Yet not everyone was so willing to forgive. Recall, the father had *two* sons.

> Now his older son was in the field. And as he came and drew near to the house, he heard music and dancing. So he called one of the servants and asked what these things meant. And he said to him, "Your brother has come, and because he has received him safe and sound, your father has killed the fatted calf."
>
> But he was angry and would not go in. Therefore his father came out and pleaded with him. So he answered and said to his father, "Lo, these many years I have been serving you; I never transgressed your commandment at any time; and yet you never gave me a young goat, that I might make merry with my friends. But as soon as this son of yours came, who has devoured your livelihood with harlots, you killed the fatted calf for him."

> And he said to him, "Son, you are always with me, and all that I have is yours. It was right that we should make merry and be glad, for your brother was dead and is alive again, and was lost and is found" (verses 25-32).

The older son represents condemnation in this parable. While his brother had been living recklessly, he had been faithfully working. He had a relationship with his dad and enjoyed all the comforts and blessings of being with his father. But here, he represents condemnation.

I want you to notice that condemnation is not only rooted in your past. It's rooted in unforgiveness. Unforgiveness also leads to condemnation.

If you are living as though you are condemned, you're not receiving the forgiveness that's available in Christ. And if you're condemning others, like the older son in this parable, then you're not extending that forgiveness. It is a sad, twisted way to live your life, a life that passes so quickly.

We can witness it in the people around us, or even in ourselves. People who are bitter immediately pull you into past offenses that occurred to them. For example, they may say something like, "Well, did you hear about what this person did to me?" And you may reply, "Did that happen recently?" Now, they've captured some momentum in their spiral. They likely reply, "No, no. But they probably did the same thing to you too. They probably..." If this sounds like you, you need to forgive and you need to move on.

The Bible commands us to forgive one another (Colossians 3:13). Only forgiveness will release you from bitterness. Do you want to be released? Forgive...and forgive...and forgive some more.

When you choose not to forgive, you become stuck in your hurt, your pain, or your failure. Those who do not make it a practice to forgive stand out in obvious ways. They stay in one place, unwilling to move forward. They tend to whine and complain, tainting their relationships with others. The Bible tells us that the root of bitterness defiles many (Hebrews 12:15). Unfortunately, it's all too common in the body of Christ.

Put yourself in the younger son's place. Coming back to God, you bring your past with you, but you also can't do anything to change it. You come to Him broken because of your past. You need to learn how to live in your Father's favor because the Father forgives the repentant.

Isn't that a wonderful thought? The Father forgives the repentant. And you wouldn't be repentant if it wasn't for the work of the Spirit of God in your life. Therefore, it's a work that begins with Him and ends with Him. And we get to be a part of it. The very fact that you want to say you're sorry is His Spirit convicting you, calling you, and drawing you into the future, not the past. And the day that you say, "I'm sick of my sin, and I hate it," is the day when you agree with the always active, convicting, and finished work of Jesus Christ in your life.

But we also must realize, the older brother is there. In Christ, you're relieved. You're free. You come home, and Dad—God the Father—is there. But so is your big brother. Dad is the picture of forgiveness. And the big brother, the picture of condemnation.

The big brother of condemnation doesn't need to present itself as another person in your life. Your big brother could be in your own head. Why? Because, at times, we're unwilling to receive God's forgiveness. Let me put it a different way: Sometimes we refuse to forgive ourselves.

Now, I know the modern world has twisted that idea. The world will tell you that you can't love others until you love yourself. When the world says to forgive yourself, they speak of pampering yourself, taking care of yourself, and putting yourself first. They tell you that you're *the* most important person, so make sure to take care of yourself before you take care of anyone else. However, that's not a biblical definition of forgiveness. The problem is that you will love yourself too much. And that is when pride rises. The need to forgive yourself is rooted in the truth of receiving the forgiveness of God. It's not an act of power on your part but a choice to surrender, in accepting God's forgiveness.

You may be thinking, *Ed, you don't understand what I've done*. And perhaps I don't. But I can assure you that God understands. And He loves you. And He sent His Son Jesus Christ to die for you. So when you forgive yourself, it's simply you believing what God says is true about you.

There is no condemnation. The price has been paid by Jesus. And the anger, bitterness, and frustration you feel will leave when you accept God's forgiveness for your past. Receive His forgiveness so you're able to move on.

When you choose the attitude of the older brother, to not accept forgiveness for your own failures, that's called idolatry. You become a little god in your life. When you refuse to accept forgiveness, you're, in effect, saying, "I understand that God forgave me. But if I was God, I wouldn't forgive myself. I'll put myself in God's place and hold my sin against me for the rest of my life."

The release from a cycle of condemnation is surrender—agreeing that God has forgiven you in Christ Jesus. Accept and receive His forgiveness. The God of the universe who created you loves you and sent His Son Jesus Christ to die for you. God forgives the repentant. And what's left for us to do is simply say, "Thank you."

When the Father runs to embrace you, what should you do? Take the hug. It feels good. In the embrace, you rest in the thought, *I can't believe this is happening. After everything I did to Him and everything I've done*. But you know you are in the right place.

Despite what the younger son did—damaging his relationship with his dad and wasting his inheritance on sinful living—his dad not only ran to embrace him, he also threw him a party. In the father's words, "It was right that we should make merry and be glad, for your brother was dead and is alive again, and was lost and is found" (Luke 15:32). It's right to forgive the past and receive forgiveness.

Too many people want to focus on the bad, on the negative. In the sanctuary of the church where I am pastor, we have offering boxes. The sole purpose of those boxes is for receiving tithes, offerings, and prayer requests. But some people who visit the church use them as complaint boxes. They don't offer a tithe or an offering. They offer a complaint about how they don't like the carpet or couldn't find a parking space. They've come to a place where God wants to minister to them, but instead, their eyes are fixed on the carpet. Their focus is on themselves.

But when there's repentance, we should be focused on the forgiveness we receive from the Father. The world will tell you that it's all about you. But God's perspective is: No, it's not about you. It's about My Son, Jesus.

The enemy loves to move our eyes off the main thing. And sometimes, we gladly cooperate. Don't get distracted from what's important. Keep your eyes on Jesus and keep forgetting and forgiving your past. It's a practice you will continually need to do.

If you hear a song that reminds you of your past, choose to forget and forgive. If you see something on social media that brings your past front and center in your mind, choose to forget and forgive. Make a conscious choice to focus on Jesus. Tell yourself, *I'm not going back there. I've been freed in Jesus Christ. I'm looking forward.*

God will help you to receive the embrace of the Father—to receive His love and forgiveness—and to keep your focus on Him.

FORSAKING YOUR PAST

After forgetting your past and forgiving your past, you need to forsake your past.

The Bible gives us very practical instructions for life. My desire is that you trust the Bible. It's not only God's love letter to you, revealing a loving, caring God. It's also God's manual for living life.

And in Psalm 103, we learn about God's heart toward us as born-again believers:

> Bless the LORD, O my soul; and all that is within me, bless His holy name! Bless the LORD, O my soul, and forget not all His benefits: who forgives all your iniquities, who heals all your diseases, who redeems your life from destruction, who crowns you with lovingkindness and tender mercies, who satisfies your mouth with good things, so that your youth is renewed like the eagle's. The LORD executes righteousness and justice for all who are oppressed. He made known His ways to Moses, His acts to the children of Israel. The LORD is merciful and gracious, slow to anger, and abounding in mercy. He will not always strive with us, nor will He keep His anger forever. He has not dealt with us according to our sins, nor punished us according to our iniquities (Psalm 103:1-10).

At this point in the psalm, I can hear a hearty amen.

This psalm reveals something important about justice. When you feel a sense of injustice, you often possess a desire for wanting justice to be served to the perpetrator. Yet, when it comes to yourself—when you are the perpetrator—you don't want justice, do you? I know I don't want justice. I don't ask God to execute justice for the wrongs I've committed. If I did, I'd be judged according to my iniquities and my failures. I don't want justice. I want Jesus.

I want Jesus for me. And I should want Jesus for others. Even for those who have hurt me or who are still hurting me. I want Jesus to heal and change us. What I really want is mercy.

Psalm 103 shows us that God's heart toward us is not justice. He has not dealt with us according to our sins. He has not punished us according to our iniquities. Not only that, but as you continue reading the psalm, you find an amazing truth:

> For as the heavens are high above the earth, so great is His mercy toward those who fear Him; as far as the east is from the west, so far has He removed our transgressions from us. As a father pities his children, so the LORD pities those who fear Him. For He knows our frame; He remembers that we are dust (verses 11-14).

As born-again believers, God forgives and forsakes our sins because Jesus paid the penalty for them on the cross. And we need to receive His forgiveness and forsake them too. The word *forsake* literally means to let it go, to let it sink or drop. God separates us from our sins.

Not only that, the Bible repeatedly declares that God will not forsake *you*. Jesus will never leave nor forsake you (Hebrews 13:5). Meaning, God will never let you sink. He'll never drop you. You cannot be separated from Him.

"The LORD is merciful and gracious, slow to anger, and abounding in mercy" (Psalm 103:8). He doesn't treat us as our sin deserves. Instead, He promises, "I forgive you. I will cast your sin far away." In Psalm 103:12, that is what the word *remove* means.[2] God casts our sin as far as the east is from the west.

Forsake your past. Let it sink. Let it drop. Stop letting the past be an excuse for your inactivity today.

I know some of you have experienced horrendous things. Painful things. But I'm so thankful they are now in the past. They're over. It's done. Even if they happened when you weren't a Christian, God was for you, not against you. He was tenderly loving you, drawing you to Himself, washing you, and changing you. God took away that little root of bitterness and comforted you in your pain. He gave you that one good night's sleep, or that good week or month of rest and calm. And then, the month became a year. God brings peace from those experiences.

Yet the enemy always wants to use the past as an excuse for your inactivity today. Don't succumb to that. The past isn't holding you back. But you might be holding on to your past. Let it go. Let it sink. Let God begin to do a work.

It reminds me of a small child with a toy. When a kid gets hold of a toy, they become superhuman. Inevitably, the time will come to put the toy away or to let another child play with it, and you become hard-pressed to pry the kid's fingers off it. As soon as you get one finger free, they grip harder and they grab the toy with their other hand. They won't let go.

You may be holding on to your past that tightly. The Holy Spirit is trying to pry your fingers off of it. Let go. Let it sink. Forsake it.

Forsaking is a little different than forgetting, isn't it? Forgetting happens in your mind. Forsaking is a posture in your life. It's where you say, "I'm letting it go. I'm letting it sink. I'm not going to hold on to it any longer." When you forsake your past, you let it sink into the sea of forgetfulness. You are right here in the present, and you are separating yourself from your past.

As we've already learned, "there is therefore now no condemnation" (Romans 8:1). *Right now.* Walking in the flesh, in condemnation, is regression—going backward and becoming spiritually dead. But for those who walk in the Spirit, the motion is forward. It's progression. It's spiritually alive.

GOD ENABLES YOU TO FORGET, FORGIVE, AND FORSAKE

You may think it's impossible to forget, forgive, and forsake your past. But God is into doing the impossible. What's impossible with man is possible with God. And the commands of God always come with His ability to enable you to follow through.

I know some of you reading this may be overwhelmed by the possibility. Some of you are in a spiritual prison, or even a physical one. If you're physically imprisoned, you know you did something you wish you hadn't done. You've got a mark on your record. And you can think it's impossible to follow through with what you have before you. But even in a spiritual prison, you feel shackled and held back. Others around you may not be aware of your condition, but like one who is held back physically, you feel like there's no future.

Listen, the power of God is greater than your inability. Other believers can help guide you, but ultimately, you must partner with the Lord to see it through. I know as a pastor, all I can do is teach you the Bible—lay it before you, encourage you, and exhort you. It's up to you to act on it.

If you believe the Lord's truths and obey His commands, crazy and wonderful changes will take place in your life. You will be spiritually free. However, if you sit around upset—arguing with your pastor, the Bible, and ultimately, with God—you're going to stay in the same place. And it's only going to get worse. The wages of sin is always death. You can't escape it.

Let me show you an example of how God enables you when you step out in faith to do what He commands you to do. In Luke 6, there was a man with a withered hand who had an encounter with Jesus:

> It happened on another Sabbath, also, that He entered the synagogue and taught. And a man was there whose right hand was withered. So the scribes and Pharisees watched Him closely, whether He would heal on the Sabbath, that they might find an accusation against Him. But He knew their thoughts, and said to the man who had the withered hand, "Arise and stand here." And he arose and stood (verses 6-8).

First of all, I think God is very gracious to this man. Jesus told the man with the withered hand to do something that he could actually do. Get up and come over. The man had to process that for a second. But you know how fast your mind works—*My legs are fine; I can stand up and walk*. Boom, it happens that fast. And he did what Jesus told him to do.

And that's how it is with you too. There are many things in your life that you likely have no problem doing. Get up on Sunday morning. Go to church. Study the Word. Pray. Read your Bible. Share the gospel. And you say, "Yes, yes, yes. I can do those things. I'll be at church. I'll read God's Word. I'll pray." It's all so wonderful and joyous. Jesus tells you, "Arise and stand here." And you think, *No problem. I'll get up and stand. I'll come to you, Jesus. No problem. I can do that.*

But then He says, "Okay, I want you to forget your past. I want you to forgive your past. I want you to forsake your past." And you tell yourself, *I can't do that*. You come to a halt.

Let's see what else Jesus asked the man to do.

> Jesus said to them, "I will ask you one thing: Is it lawful on the Sabbath to do good or to do evil, to save life or to destroy?" And when He had looked around at them all, He said to the man, "Stretch out your hand" (verses 9-10).

Do you know what that was? An impossibility. The man couldn't stretch out his hand. It was withered. We must understand the weight of this request.

That's how you may be feeling about the idea of forgetting, forgiving, and forsaking your past. You may be thinking, *It's impossible. I'll come to church. I'll read the Bible. I'll love God and serve Him. Keep telling me to do things I can do. But don't tell me to do what I can't do.*

For some, you argue or wrestle with the truth. It's hard to receive it. It takes a little time. Maybe you are like Jesus' disciple Thomas.

Thomas needed time. He needed to see something. He had to feel something. And Jesus was gracious to Thomas. Jesus said, "Reach your finger here, and look at My hands; and reach your hand here, and put it into My side. Do not be unbelieving, but believing" (John 20:27). I'm grateful He didn't rebuke Thomas. Jesus gave him what he needed.

Yet in Luke 6, when Jesus told the man with the withered hand, "Stretch out your hand," the very next sentence says, "And he did so" (Luke 6:10). Looking at that verse in your Bible, you will see Jesus' command, then there's a quotation mark, a space, and the word *and.* In that small moment, the man could have responded, "No way. This guy doesn't know what He's talking about. My hand has been withered forever. Look at it. It doesn't move. I haven't moved this hand for years. This is impossible. I won't do it."

But the Bible does not tell us about a lack of faith from this man. Instead, notice what it says,

> "Stretch out your hand." And he did so (verse 10).

What do you mean, "he did so"? The man's hand was withered. Consider this, there's no pause. Stretch out your hand; he did so. Just like that. Why? Because in the breath of the command of God comes His enabling power for you to do what He tells you to do. It's not your strength. It's not your wisdom. It's your faith that makes you well.

This is a powerful realization for us. In those times when hope is withering up like the man's hand, when you're paralyzed and struggling, know this: As Jesus enters in, He is always drawn toward the one who is hurting the most. He's not so interested in the mockers, the people who play games, and the ones who want to test Him. Jesus knows your thoughts. Right now, the fact that Jesus knows your thoughts could make you feel good or uneasy. But He's always on the lookout for the one who is hurting the most. In Luke 6, He found this man and He gave a command. And it was an absolute impossibility for the man to obey Jesus' command on his own.

I don't know if you've ever lived with something that's so hurtful, painful, and difficult that it's on your mind the second you wake up. And it's on your mind when you fall asleep. Sometimes, it's so pervasive that you dream about it. You can't even get away from it in your sleep. No doubt the disability in this man's life was something that was always on his mind. He must have tried to send a signal from his brain to his hand a million times before, hoping that his body would oblige. And sure, he must have resolved that he would live with this for his whole life. But that doesn't mean he didn't deal with it every day.

So when Jesus gave the man the command, he could've said no. But he didn't. He decided to obey. And just like the man, as you purpose in your heart to obey, God will meet you in that place. Let it be your story that when God says to you, "Forget, forgive, and forsake your past," the next sentence is, "And she did so"; or "And he did so."

If you choose to obey, God will show up in a powerful way. The moment that God commands an impossible thing, He will enable you to follow through.

Although the past keeps coming back, don't hold on to it. Let it go. Forget the past. Don't dwell on it. Forgive the past, both enjoying the forgiveness of the Father and extending the forgiveness of the Father to others. Forsake the past, let it go, leave it behind.

We need to obey God—to step out in faith—to forget our past, forgive our past, and forsake our past. Release your past and move forward. As you make that decision of obedience, little by little, the Holy Spirit will affirm that response in your life and strengthen you. Whether it's your recent past or a distant one, God's life-giving power will enable you.

REFLECTION/DISCUSSION QUESTIONS

1. What is something from your past that you need to forget? Make the conscious choice to release it to the Lord, believe that His promises are true, and reach forward to the future.
2. What is something that you need to forgive? Whether its cause is someone else or yourself, receive the forgiveness that is available in Christ.
3. What is something that is keeping you stuck in the past and holding you back from how God wants to use you today? What is a step that you can take today to move forward?
4. What is something in your life that is withered or dead that you would like to allow Jesus to breathe new life into?

5

DEALING WITH FORGIVENESS

A number of years ago in a small town in Spain, a man and his teenage son had a very painful argument. The argument led to a falling out between them. Deep feelings of bitterness, resentment, and unforgiveness followed. The son launched out on his own, angry and upset. He left his home in the countryside and went to the city.

As time passed, the father regretted the falling out. He sensed the mistakes he had made in how he had treated his son. So he searched for his boy, day and night. Several months passed, and the father still wasn't able to find him. In one last-ditch effort, he placed the following ad in the classified section of a Madrid newspaper:

> *Dear Paco, Meet me in front of the newspaper office at noon. All is forgiven. I love you. Your father.*

By twelve o'clock the next day, there were more than 800 men named Paco gathered outside the newspaper building. Every one of them was looking for forgiveness from his father.[1]

There's a desperate need for forgiveness today. If such an advertisement was put out on social media with your name on it, saying forgiveness is available, would you show up looking for the forgiveness that you never received?

In the previous chapter, we learned how important it is to forgive your past—how you need to forgive yourself by accepting God's forgiveness. Another component of forgiving your past is to forgive others.

Forgiveness is so needed. Families are broken. Marriages are dissolved. Painful circumstances continue to happen, resulting in separation and division. We live in a difficult time. The Bible warned us: In the last days, the hearts of many will grow cold (Matthew 24:12). And that includes believers. It's possible for our hearts to grow cold and hard toward the things of God.

When you hold on to resentment, anger, and bitterness, you're living with an unforgiving spirit. Unforgiveness continues to weaken the church, divide families, and erode the effectiveness of believers' lives. Damage, pain, and separation are rooted in the sin of unforgiveness. And yes, the Bible declares it to be a sin.

FOUR REASONS YOU SHOULD FORGIVE

Jesus taught His followers, "If you forgive those who sin against you, your heavenly Father will forgive you. But if you refuse to forgive others, your Father will not forgive your sins" (Matthew 6:14-15 NLT).

Forgiving others is nonnegotiable. It's not a choice for the believer. Jesus told us to forgive as we've been forgiven. If you aren't convinced, following are four reasons you must forgive. These insights on forgiveness were developed from Craig Caster's workbook on forgiveness.[2]

1. Forgiveness is commanded by God.

Forgiveness is a command. And obedience isn't optional. As we saw above, in Matthew 6:14-15, Jesus instructed us to forgive. He taught the same thing in Mark 11: "But when you are praying, first forgive anyone you are holding a grudge against, so that your Father in heaven will forgive your sins, too" (Mark 11:25 NLT). It's a command.

2. Forgiveness reflects Jesus.

Forgiveness reflects the very image of Jesus Christ. When Jesus was crucified on the cross for our sins, He wasn't crucified alone. Two criminals were executed with Him, and they witnessed an astonishing moment. The Bible tells us,

> Two others, both criminals, were led out to be executed with him. When they came to a place called The Skull, they nailed him to the cross. And the criminals were also crucified—one on his right and one on his left. Jesus said, "Father, forgive them, for they don't know what they are doing." And the soldiers gambled for his clothes by throwing dice (Luke 23:32-34 NLT).

Jesus asked the Father to forgive what seems to be unforgivable—the crucifixion of His only begotten Son. Jesus petitioned the Father on behalf of His own executioners. And at least one person recognized the weight of this, the criminal who asked Jesus to remember him in His kingdom (verses 39-43). When we forgive, we reflect Jesus.

3. Forgiveness breaks down strongholds.

Forgiveness breaks down strongholds in our lives. When you forgive, you experience healing in your hurting heart. Forgiveness is the one major antidote to bitterness. Obedience to forgive brings freedom and enables you to start over in a relationship by the grace and mercy of God.

In Genesis, you can read about an example of restoration in the life of Joseph. His brothers had sold him into slavery out of jealousy (Genesis 37). Later, their positions of power were reversed. Joseph was the second in command in Egypt, with control over the nation's food supply during a drought. Joseph's brothers came to him for food (41:39–42:7). Joseph could have been bitter over what they had done to him. But he wasn't. He forgave and helped them (45:3-15). And because his brothers were repentant, Joseph's forgiveness paved the way for restoration in their relationship. Forgiveness brings freedom.

4. Forgiveness relieves the offender's guilt.

Forgiveness loosens the stranglehold of guilt in the offender. That person no longer needs to rehearse their sin and carry it unforgiven by someone else. They become released by love and kindness.

As the Bible tells us,

> God can point to us in all future ages as examples of the incredible wealth of his grace and kindness toward us, as shown in all he has done for us who are united with Christ Jesus (Ephesians 2:7 NLT).

God always points us to the wealth and favor of His kindness toward us. Forgiveness brings freedom to everyone involved.

Remember, we forgive because God has forgiven us in Christ. We didn't deserve to be forgiven. Nor did we earn that forgiveness. In turn, we must forgive others even if they don't deserve it. When we forgive, it relieves the oppressive burden of guilt. If Jesus had not extended kindness and forgiveness to sinners, we would forever exist in the stranglehold of guilt, sin, and darkness.

Let me remind you that *forgiveness* and *reconciliation* are two distinct things. Often, any confusion that surrounds the subject of forgiveness stems from confusing these two things as being one.

Forgiveness is an act of obedience in which you release a debt. You acknowledge that someone hurt you. And then, you make a conscious decision to release it and let it go.

You can forgive someone even if you can't tell them you have. For example, sometimes the unforgiveness in your life is tied to someone who has already passed away. Whether the person who you are extending forgiveness to is currently in your life or not, you can release that person daily before the Lord when feelings of bitterness show up in your heart.

Different than forgiveness, reconciliation is usually a natural byproduct of forgiveness. But reconciliation requires an additional step by the person being forgiven. That additional step is repentance. Without repentance, there can be no restoration of the relationship. That's why the process of reconciliation can be frustrating.

When repentance doesn't occur, you may be left thinking, *I've forgiven them, but nothing has changed.* But that is not entirely true. By extending forgiveness, *you* are free. That is a huge change. Don't discount the fact that you are free. And if the other person hasn't repented, keep forgiving any new wrongs while you're praying for repentance to occur.

/////

These principles are very powerful. And they are good to revisit from time to time because the passage of time always brings new circumstances and interactions with others. There are always new hurts. There are always new difficulties. And there are always new thoughts that are brought to mind on how to relate and respond to them. The enemy is relentless. Do not live by the flesh; instead, live in the Spirit.

Forgiveness is essential. It's a command. It's something that you're able to extend. And when you do, you will be free.

A PICTURE OF FORGIVENESS

Let's look at a beautiful picture of forgiveness from the life of King Jehoiachin. At the time, Jerusalem had fallen, and the Babylonians put King Jehoiachin—the second-to-the-last of the kings of Judah—in prison. King Jehoiachin was in prison for 37 years.

During those 37 years, the ruler of Babylon, King Nebuchadnezzar, pridefully talked about *his* great power and *his* great possessions, only to be humbled by God. King Nebuchadnezzar declared, "Is not this great Babylon, that I have built for a royal dwelling by my mighty power and for the honor of my majesty?" (Daniel 4:30).

While the words were still in King Nebuchadnezzar's mouth, God gave him a mind of a beast. Imagine, the king of the known world—who had conquered Judah and taken all its possessions and people captive—was now like a beast. And he remained like that for seven years.

His son, Evil-Merodach, took his place to rule Babylon. Then, at the end of his seven years of madness, Nebuchadnezzar ended up praising God, returned to the throne, discovered the evil of his son's rule, and threw his son into prison.

But then Nebuchadnezzar died. And his son got out of prison and had the chance to rule again. Let's look at what happened when Evil-Merodach got another chance.

> It came to pass in the thirty-seventh year of the captivity of Jehoiachin king of Judah, in the twelfth month, on the twenty-fifth day of the month, that Evil-Merodach king of Babylon, in the first year of his reign, lifted up the head of Jehoiachin king of Judah and brought him out of prison. And he spoke kindly to him and gave him a more prominent seat than those of the kings who were with him in Babylon. So Jehoiachin changed from his prison garments, and he ate bread regularly before the king all the days of his life. And as for his provisions, there was a regular ration given him by the king of Babylon, a portion for each day until the day of his death, all the days of his life (Jeremiah 52:31-34).

One of the first things that Nebuchadnezzar's son did was to go to the prison and bring out Jehoiachin. He gave him a kingship higher than all the kingships of the Babylonian kingdom. Imagine that. It's difficult to think about being imprisoned for 37 years. It must have been a weird feeling for Jehoiachin to be released after all that time. I'm sure it was a very awkward adjustment. He had once been the king of Judah. Then, he spent 37 years in confinement, and in an instant, he was freed.

Over the years, I've found that many people get used to their captivity. They get used to where they are—to their sinful habits and the patterns of their flesh. Many have made unforgiveness their best friend. They've become friends with bitterness. They have more conversations with themselves about the people they're upset with than spending true prayer time with the Lord. People get used to their captivity. They become accustomed to being defined by their failures instead of being defined by the power of God.

Sadly, some people would rather stay in their captivity than move into the freedom that the Lord gives through His grace and mercy. Remaining in captivity is not the will of Jesus Christ for you. He wants to set you free. In a very real way, you are set free as you take the steps of forgiveness. There's newness and forgiveness in Jesus.

It requires a choice. In response to the forgiveness extended by Jesus, you can forgive. Or, you can live in the shadow of your own condemnation. Because the anger and frustration that result from unforgiveness lead to regret—which often leads to condemnation—that regret will stifle the very life-giving power of Jesus Christ out of us.

You need to forgive yourself, and you need to forgive others. I know it's a painful process. God's forgiveness and your forgiveness don't eliminate the consequences of sin. Consequences come out of our failures. And they come about from other people's sinful actions. Those consequences remind us of what we did or what happened and it becomes very difficult. Sometimes, God is very gracious and minimizes the consequences. Yet other times, we feel their full weight. In addition, someone could respond to you sinfully in light of a consequence in your life, and you also have to deal with that. It's painful.

But the place of abiding in Jesus—of resting in Him, receiving His forgiveness, and forgiving others—is a place of freedom. Like Jehoiachin, you may have a hard time not living in captivity. You may find it difficult to live in the newness of life. If we can't forgive or receive forgiveness, we can't move on. We can't move forward. In unforgiveness, we're stuck. Unforgiveness equates to a prison of misery. Unforgiveness is often the reason we're not making progress in our relationship with God.

In Jeremiah 52, we observe the king of Babylon. He's not even a believer. He doesn't love God. Yet, he shows more forgiveness here than most people give to others. Here we learn of a greater King. We learn about the King of kings. He is greater than this generous king from Babylon. The King of kings descended into our prison of desperation and darkness. When we were lost and without any hope, wandering around blinded to our own sins, He died on the cross for those sins, so we could be forgiven.

There are six things that we discover about forgiveness from the release of King Jehoiachin.

1. Jehoiachin was brought out.

The king was the person who brought Jehoiachin out of prison. The Bible says, "Evil-Merodach king of Babylon, in the first year of his reign, lifted up the head of Jehoiachin king of Judah and brought him out of prison" (Jeremiah 52:31).

Evil-Merodach brought him out. The king didn't send a messenger. He didn't send a servant. And he didn't have the prison guard release him. He chose to do it himself.

That's interesting to me. The king had been in captivity himself.

Evil-Merodach was elevated to the throne after his father died. For all intents and purposes, he was *the* leader of the known world at the time. And he took it upon himself to go back down into the very prison that he had just been released from to release King Jehoiachin.

And that's what God has done for us. The Creator of the universe Himself has forgiven us and set us free. He didn't send a messenger. He didn't send an angel. He didn't send a pastor or a priest. God Himself came down and delivered you from your prison of sin and darkness. God is ready to forgive all the rotten things we've ever done. All our sins have been buried, washed away, blotted out, and forgiven by Jesus Christ. He came Himself.

Jesus set aside His divine prerogatives and came to release us from our sins. And we can be sure, "If the Son sets you free, you are truly free" (John 8:36 NLT). It's a done deal. Nobody can second-guess it. The King has the authority, and He came and took care of it Himself. I love that.

2. Jehoiachin was comforted.

The king of Babylon comforted Jehoiachin. It says that "he spoke kindly to him and gave him a more prominent seat" (Jeremiah 52:32).

You know, the church of Jesus could use more kindness. Obviously, the world needs it as well. But in the church, we could be kinder and gentler with one another. We could cut each other some slack, especially when we are aware that a brother or sister is only recently emerging out of captivity.

The king showed Jehoiachin kindness. I'm sure that after 37 years of imprisonment, Jehoiachin was discouraged, depressed, and hopeless. He likely had resigned himself to life in prison. But the king of Babylon encouraged him and gave him hope.

In the same way, God comes to us personally, lifts our heads, and gives us hope. We're forgiven. And we're set free. But we might be lacking confidence. Or we may be in a weakened state.

Believers are surrounded by people who are running this race with us. It may not appear like you are in the lead, but support and encouragement is found in the pack. There's a guy who overcame this, and a gal who overcame that. The church is filled with overcomers. We shouldn't be a church filled with people who only offer hypercritical judgment and finger-pointing. We should be a church filled with freedom.

That's not to say that we don't speak to and address difficulties. It's not that we don't confront sin. Of course, we do. But it must be done with kindness and gentleness.

In Galatians 6, we see a New Testament illustration of what's happening in Jeremiah 52. And I pray that you would take this to heart and become better at it. It reads,

> Brethren, if a man is overtaken in any trespass, you who are spiritual restore such a one in a spirit of gentleness, considering yourself lest you also be tempted. Bear one another's burdens, and so fulfill the law of Christ (Galatians 6:1-2).

Doesn't a heavy burden lose some of its weight when it is shared? Your burden is lightened when someone comes along to help you carry the load. The Bible says to bear one another's burdens "for if anyone thinks himself to be something"—that's where pride comes in—"when he is nothing"—this is where humility comes in—"he deceives himself. But let each one examine his own work, and then he will have rejoicing in himself alone, and not in another. For each one shall bear his own load" (Galatians 6:3-5).

This practice is an indicator that shows where you're at spiritually. We all like to say we're spiritual; but do you want to *know* if you're spiritual? Evaluate how you respond when you see someone overtaken by a trespass. Because, if you're spiritual, you'll want to rush in and restore them.

The word *restore* comes from a Greek word that, in the medical community, refers to the putting together of a broken bone.[3] When a bone is fractured, it gets reset to heal. There is an adage I've heard that says, once a bone is set after a break, it never breaks in the same place again. Perhaps, it could be an exception. Perhaps, the bone truly becomes stronger. But imagine that image in our lives. Our very worst time can become the best time for our transformation in the hands of the Lord. Certainly, it takes patience and we will need healing. In our worst place, we can't conceive how God could bring anything good out of it. But He does.

God restores and rebuilds. He helps us. And God lifts our heads. He gives us hope as we're forgiven and set free. As it says in Psalm 3, "You, O Lord, are a shield for me, my glory and the One who lifts up my head. I cried to the Lord with my voice, and He heard me from His holy hill" (verses 3-4). There's no longer a reason to hang our heads and condemn ourselves because we have freedom. The God of the universe is in the business of restoration.

In our daily lives, we should never underestimate the power of offering a kind word, an encouraging text, a helpful note, a quick email, a phone call, or a knock on the door to others. Those are all ways in which we can show kindness. We can show them that we value the relationship that we have with them. Never undervalue the effect your kindness may have on their soul.

For instance, if you're driving to work one morning, listening to a song, and an encouraging thought about someone comes into your mind, act on it when you get to work. Maybe during your devotions or while you are reading the Bible, a scripture pops out at you and sticks in your mind. You don't quite understand it at the time because it doesn't relate to anything currently going on in your life, but it really sticks out. It's as if it jumped off the page. I assure you, if you meditate on that scripture, God will bring a purpose to it. Perhaps, that purpose is to inspire you to connect with someone you haven't seen at church in a while—a relative or others who have crossed your path. Don't underestimate the power of kindness and encouragement.

I'm sure you've experienced the power of a kind word. You've also experienced the power of a word that wasn't fitly spoken. When we yield to God's Spirit, the kind word (rather than the misplaced one) will flow through us. The fruit of the Spirit is love, joy, peace, patience, kindness, goodness, faithfulness, gentleness, and self-control (Galatians 5:22-23).

Evil-Merodach didn't release Jehoiachin, and then lay a heavy guilt trip on him. The king didn't ask him a series of accusing questions. He comforted him.

3. Jehoiachin was exalted.

The king exalted Jehoiachin. Not only did he speak kindly, the king of Babylon "gave [Jehoiachin] a more prominent seat than those of the kings who were with him in Babylon" (Jeremiah 52:32). The king restored Jehoiachin's life to what it had been before the enemy ripped him off.

Doesn't that reflect the work of God? God wants to restore what the enemy has stolen from you. He wants to bring you back and place your feet on a solid rock. He wants you to walk forward with Him.

As the psalmist said, "My feet had almost stumbled; my steps had nearly slipped" (Psalm 73:2). The psalmist's statement means that it was almost over for him. *I was that close. I almost didn't come back.* And yet, he did come back. He came back stronger. He didn't get caught up in a series of slips. Later in the psalm, he extols the power of God to bring him off the ledge (Psalm 73:23-26).

Some use that phrase from time to time. When we help someone who is in a great crisis, afterward, we'll say something like, "We had the privilege of talking them off the ledge." The phrase really does speak of someone being at the end of their rope. They cannot envision anything more for them.

That is often the place of suicidal thoughts. It's a place of deep hopelessness. And whether it's real or imagined, no matter. The person feels it either way. It's 100 percent real to them. We must meet people where they're at. (If you are having suicidal thoughts even as you read this, please ask for help right away. Call a friend. Or call a hotline by dialing 988. There is help available right now.)

Some of the worst advice to a person in crisis is, "Oh, you shouldn't be feeling that. Why are you feeling that way?" Don't say that! Speak to people in their pain. Go down into the pit with them and escort them out. Remind them of God's power and the hope found in Him. Comfort them. Speak kindly. Lift up their heads. Point them toward Jesus so God can begin a work in their lives. Then their testimony will be, *My feet almost slipped. But God was faithful.*

Because we're merely human, we deal with our own sin. In addition, we are affected by everyone else's sin and the consequences of living in this painful world. Much of the world lives in opposition to God. They hate God and have no morality about them. They're motivated only by their own greed and selfishness. This can be overwhelming.

Have resentment and bitterness set in to your life? Have you resigned yourself to the thought that life cannot be restored, that it's impossible to rebound from a painful situation? I want to meet you with a message of hope. I know many who have come down off the ledge. And we rejoice for it.

God has the power to bring you off the ledge. God forgives you and He restores you. God's work in your life will be tremendous and breathtaking. Don't overlook the part of Psalm 23 where it tells us that our good Shepherd—Jesus—restores our soul (Psalm 23:3).

4. The king clothed Jehoiachin.

The king of Babylon gave Jehoiachin new clothing. Not only was Jehoiachin brought out, comforted, and exalted, he was given new clothes. The Bible says, "So Jehoiachin changed from his prison garments" (Jeremiah 52:33). He was released from prison, encouraged, and given a throne. And then, he put on a royal robe.

Jehoiachin had been in prison for 37 years. He was a king who was known as an enemy of Babylon. And what does he receive? A royal robe.

Think about the great work that God does in our lives. He restores our nature. He restores our integrity. He restores our character. And He sees us in Christ. He views us wearing the robes of righteousness. We don't come to Him with our own beggarly garments, desperately trying to cover ourselves.

The Bible speaks of God taking away the garment of sadness and giving us the garment of praise. Jesus came

> to console those who mourn in Zion, to give them beauty for ashes, the oil of joy for mourning, the garment of praise for the spirit of heaviness; that they may be called trees of righteousness, the planting of the LORD, that He may be glorified (Isaiah 61:3).

During His ministry, Jesus shared a parable about a wedding, and there was a man who didn't have the right garments for the occasion. To attend, you needed to be given the right garments from the king (Matthew 22:11-12). As a follower of Jesus Christ, you are robed with the right garments. You're not wearing prison garments anymore. There are no longer shackles on your arms.

5. Jehoiachin was favored.

The king favored Jehoiachin. The Bible says, "He ate bread regularly before the king all the days of his life" (Jeremiah 52:33). Jehoiachin ate like a king for the rest of his life. He no longer had to eat prison bread. Instead, he was served the bread of a king. And this all changed for him in an instant. Evil-Merodach didn't abandon

Jehoiachin. In fact, by his invitation to eat at his table, he wanted him to know that they would be friends forever.

When God forgives us, He draws us to Himself in relationship. Your relationship with God, by faith in Jesus Christ, is not a religious experience. The people on the stage where you worship don't do all the work for you. The pastor who preaches from the pulpit doesn't take care of everything you need.

Religion offers you the sense that you can never approach God. You're never good enough. You'll never make it. In religion, you work hard, give in abundance, need a human intercessor, and go through the motions. Then, *maybe* you'll make it to heaven. You only find out after you die.

That's religion. Religion puts burdens on you. It places a barrier between you and God. It requires the opposite of what God teaches us in His Word.

God comes to you personally. And He continually invites you to His table. You enjoy what the King enjoys. And He is the one who places you there. You don't take it upon yourself. You recognize the weak and beggarly condition of your life.

You will never experience a relationship with Jesus Christ until you understand how far you are from Him. The Bible says that we've been separated from God by sin. There is no connection between man and God. We have all sinned and fallen short of God's glory, His perfection (Romans 3:23).

In other words, no one is perfect. In our flesh, we make allowances and excuses because of this state we are in. But it's a serious condition to recognize. If you acknowledge that you're not perfect, you're saying, "I have sinned against you, God. I have failed to live up to Your standard. I've failed to live the way You want me to live."

God is our Creator. He created us in His image. The purpose of our lives is to honor Him. And we're alive on the earth to make God known to those around us. That's why we're here. We once lived for ourselves, damaging our own and others' lives.

We live in a culture that says, "Do whatever you want as long as it doesn't hurt anyone." Those who believe that philosophy forget that you can hurt yourself with your actions, disintegrating your soul.

An episode in my life comes to mind, one that happened before I started following Jesus. I remember going to jail and, while in custody, being violently beaten up. I was injured severely enough that they called my dad to pick me up. But they didn't tell him the extent of how bad my injuries were.

You must understand something about my dad. My dad is in the presence of the Lord now, but when he was on this earth, he wasn't a man that displayed much emotion. He wasn't a man of much expression. He was a calm, quiet, and reliable guy. He loved his family. He was a faithful provider. My dad was not a man of great highs. And he certainly wasn't a man of great lows. My family never saw him get very angry. And likewise, we never saw him incredibly happy either.

I hardly ever recall seeing my dad cry. But on that day, when my dad picked me up from the police department, all bloodied and beaten up, he began weeping over the condition of his son. I remember it like it was yesterday.

Our decisions can hurt us. And they can hurt the people who love us. So the world's philosophy of do whatever you want as long as it doesn't harm anyone isn't true. You can't do whatever you want because our poor decisions always end up hurting someone. We must learn to think of others more than ourselves. If you've concluded that you're not a perfect person, then there have been times when you've hurt yourself and those who love you through your actions.

And there's only one remedy. The Bible says that the wages of sin—the wages of our selfish actions—is always death (Romans 6:23a). That death is all around us. The death of relationships. The death of hope. The death of strength. The death of marriages. Not only physical death, although physical death reminds us that sin is ever with us, but death in so many other areas where sin destroys.

Although the wages of sin is death, "the gift of God is eternal life in Christ Jesus our Lord" (Romans 6:23b). The only remedy for sinners is this: Talk to God, admit that you've failed Him, and receive His forgiveness. Yes, God the Creator, knowing everything about you, extends His forgiveness to you.

Jesus says, whoever will, let him come. You don't need to clean up your life first. God has made a way of escape for you. If you turn away from your sins, God will forgive you, even right now as you read this book. It doesn't matter where you are. God is ready to forgive. The offer of salvation through Jesus Christ is available to all who will hear and come to Him.

Jesus says, if you believe, you'll be saved. If you don't believe, you'll be lost. The decision is up to you. Forgiveness is available. And to enjoy forgiveness is to come to God and be honest with Him. Tell Him about the condition of your life and receive His forgiveness.

By receiving God's forgiveness, your life will be transformed. And one day, you'll be sitting at the table of the King of kings, enjoying the wedding feast of the Lamb (Revelation 19:9).

6. Jehoiachin's future was secure.

The king secured Jehoiachin's future. Forgiveness secures the future. Jehoiachin had nothing to worry about for the rest of his life. The king assured him that he would be taken care of all his days. In Jeremiah 52:34, we learn, "As for his provisions, there was a regular ration given him by the king of Babylon, a portion for each day until the day of his death."

In Christ Jesus, you have an eternal hope that God will take care of you for the rest of your life. God has secured your future. And we've been given the promise of eternal life. *Nothing* can snatch you out of the Father's hands (John 10:29) or separate you from the love of God (Romans 8:38-39).

The greatest gift in our lives is God's forgiveness. Yet, it tends to be one of the most overlooked provisions that He gives us. We take it for granted. And when we take God's forgiveness for granted, we take our relationships for granted.

THE NEED FOR TRUE FORGIVENESS

Forgiveness that is not complete is not true forgiveness. When a person says, "I forgive you, but I'll never forget," that is not true, biblical, and loving forgiveness. It's more like saying, "Let's bury the hatchet." The blade is stuck in the ground while leaving the handle in the air, so you can grab it again at any time.

The problem with man is that our forgiveness isn't always true forgiveness. Instead of forgiving others by following God's example, we do it our own way. When we do that, we put ourselves in the position of God. We're basically saying, "If I was God, this is what I would do." We neglect to recognize that God is on the throne where He belongs. God cannot and will not be dethroned. But we can live our lives as if we are the one on the throne.

As I said, the problem with man is that our forgiveness isn't always true. We don't have a proper concept of forgiveness. We forget what true forgiveness is. We forget how God has forgiven us.

When God forgives us, we receive total, complete forgiveness. He promises to never remember our sin again (Hebrews 8:12; see also Jeremiah 31:34). Our sin is separated from us as far as the east is from the west (Psalm 103:12). You will never need to answer to God for the sin that's been placed under the blood of Jesus Christ. It's gone. You have been washed. You are cleansed.

Now, you know as well as I do that the human mind is an amazing organ that God has created. And our memories are something incredibly special. As much as we tend to forget, we also remember a lot. When we are discussing not remembering past sin again, what it really means is that you choose not to hold the sin against the person.

So it is tragic that in our relationships we will say that we forgive, but then, bring up past offenses and use them in our arguments. This practice can be especially prominent in marriages, where one spouse, or the pair, bring up the past to get their way. You must guard against this. God wants you to forgive as He forgave you. In the marriage discipleship that occurs at the church where I serve, there's a list of agreed upon guardrails that couples commit to use in their arguments that we call Fight Rules. One of those rules is: Don't use the past as a weapon. This rule is not only beneficial for marriage relationships but is equally important for every other relationship you find yourself in.

God doesn't hold our past against us. We can't compare God's forgiveness with how we forgive one another because God's forgiveness is complete. You have been justified. You are declared innocent. It's as if you've never committed the sin to begin with. God wipes the slate clean. He erases and blots out our transgressions. There's no need to look back. Press forward. God has forgiven it and wiped it away.

And we can ask God for His power to forgive. Remember, it's not something you can will yourself to do. That leads to frustration and failure. But you can say, "I surrender myself to forgive," and ask God for His help to follow through. It is "God who works in you both to will and to do for His good pleasure" (Philippians 2:13). It's God's work. It's His agape love. It's His true spiritual forgiveness. It comes from Him and flows through us.

God's forgiveness is a beautiful thing to experience. Just like King Jehoiachin, years in captivity and, in an instant, he's changed. His life is one of the many pictures in the Bible of the great power of the blood of Jesus Christ.

REFLECTION/DISCUSSION QUESTIONS

1. Do you have a personal relationship with our Lord Jesus Christ? If not, what is stopping you? Today is the day of salvation.
2. Why is forgiveness something that the Lord commands us to do?
3. Think about something that you have not forgiven in your own life. What has that done to your feelings and behaviors?
4. Understanding the difference between forgiveness and reconciliation, how does that change you and your behavior going forward?
5. Is it okay to only forgive and not to seek reconciliation? Why or why not?
6. Think about a time when someone showed you kindness. How did the Lord use that in your situation?

6

DEALING WITH YOUR ANGER

If you are going to walk in freedom from your past, you must deal with any lingering issues of sinful anger. There is a good anger. But there's also a bad anger.

There are two Greek words that are translated as *anger* in the New Testament. One means to have passion or energy. And the other means agitated or boiling.[1] So, there's a good anger and a bad anger.

Righteous anger is a God-given emotion in our lives used to move us to action. That anger arises from seeing unfairness or injustice. Also, it warns us to avoid harm in the future. That is a good anger.

Examples of this anger include David being upset over the injustice that Nathan the prophet shared with him (2 Samuel 12:5-6). And—as is commonly highlighted when discussing the topic of anger—Jesus gave us an example of righteous anger when He went into the temple and flipped over tables because the people doing business inside had defiled His Father's house (John 2:13-16). Also, we see an example of righteous anger when Paul confronts the sorcerer who was seeking to turn the proconsul of Cyprus, Sergius Paulus, away from the faith (Acts 13:6-12). Paul would not stand for someone trying to persuade someone else to disbelief. When you think of righteous anger, notice that it is an anger that stands for what is biblically correct.

I want to be clear that the anger we will be addressing in this chapter is sinful anger. Sinful anger is an outburst of wrath that the Bible calls a work of the flesh (Galatians 5:20). It's a sin. It is a bad anger. Sinful, unrighteous anger is something that we need to deal with. And it must be dealt with promptly. Although it's sinful, it has been one of the most justified and excused sins within the church.

More than 50 percent of people who go to a counselor or psychologist want help dealing with an anger issue in their lives.[2] That statistic includes both believers and unbelievers. In my own personal experience in ministering to people, I have seen that number higher. At the root of many issues that cause turmoil in your life—like division, marital trouble, and parenting struggles—is your unrighteous anger. And those issues can't be resolved unless you're willing to admit your anger is sinful and to repent from it.

Anger arises when you're offended by something. It takes hold of you when you feel like something's outside of your control. When you feel that way, you try to manipulate the situation through anger. It starts with the feeling that you've been wronged or that something is wrong. The feeling comes from a place of hurt. There are deep hurts that lead to anger. But generally, it only takes a simple offense to set it off.

For example, let's say you're driving on the highway on your way to work. You're singing a worship song to the Lord. You're meditating on the Bible teaching you heard last Sunday. You couldn't be more in tune with heaven. You're encouraged. In fact, you're so encouraged that you need to remember to keep your hands on the steering wheel because you're in the middle of driving. You're in the Spirit, enjoying what God's doing in your life.

Then, it happens. Someone cuts you off. Immediately, you feel offended. You're hurt by it, but you don't even sense the hurt. You don't acknowledge the offense because the anger wells up in you that quickly. You become a different person, and various responses follow.

Some of us will throw up our arms and hurl insults at the driver who can't even hear us. Others get so caught up in the offense that they follow the car, catch up to them, and shout at the driver through closed windows. None of those responses are going to help anything. But people do that. And, yes, even believers do that.

If that is you, after you calm down you likely ask yourself, *What was I doing?* You haven't yet accepted that it wasn't that big of a deal. You have not resolved in your mind that everything is going to be okay. Instead, you've established a habit of hurt in your reactions. When you're hurt, you want to give hurt right back. The other driver did something wrong. But rather than wondering if there was a good reason for their sudden movement, you get upset and offended, as if you own the lane or the whole highway. This is a real issue.

When you're offended, if you don't respond biblically, the problem will only get worse. The first thing that happens when you respond in the flesh is you get upset, not necessarily angry, but upset. When you don't deal with being upset, you become frustrated. Then, frustration turns into bitterness. When you reach the point of bitterness, no one can do right in your eyes. To put it into words using our illustration, now *everyone* on the road is a horrible driver. When you are bitter, you become unforgiving.

And you may wonder, *How did I get like this?* The answer is you never dealt with the original offense. You didn't take that offense to the Lord and trust His sovereignty in your life.

The way to get out of this cycle is forgiveness. Simply forgive. Release others from the debt that they owe you. And you can move forward with your life.

However, when you respond to offenses in your flesh, after many years, you can see how deep-rooted anger can become in your life. Anger is devastating. It rips apart relationships. It destroys unity. And it hurts many.

The good news is that Jesus will help you. He can replace your wrath with the fruit of the Spirit. And He wants to deliver you today. He wants you to be free from anger. He wants you to walk in the Spirit. If you're a born-again believer, He dwells in you. If you are not born again, He wants to do a work in your life when you confess your sin and surrender your life to Him.

You know as well as I do, your angry self is not getting you what you want. I have met many people who regret that the life they used to lead was full of anger. It is a life that substitutes God's blessings for hollow imposters. It's like God is laying out a whole feast before you, saying, "Come and enjoy the feast. Look at the meal I provided for you." And instead, you choose to eat a warmed-up burger that you bought last week from a fast-food restaurant. And worse, the burger has green things growing on it. God has given you everything you need to live an abundant life. And you're settling for so much less.

King Nebuchadnezzar gives us a clear example of someone who dealt with an anger issue. In Daniel 2, we read,

> In the second year of Nebuchadnezzar's reign, Nebuchadnezzar had dreams; and his spirit was so troubled that his sleep left him. Then the king gave the command to call the magicians, the astrologers, the sorcerers, and the Chaldeans to tell the king his dreams. So they came and stood before the king. And the king said to them, "I have had a dream, and my spirit is anxious to know the dream."
>
> Then the Chaldeans spoke to the king in Aramaic, "O king, live forever! Tell your servants the dream, and we will give the interpretation."
>
> The king answered and said to the Chaldeans, "My decision is firm: if you do not make known the dream to me, and its interpretation, you shall be cut in pieces, and your houses shall be made an ash heap" (verses 1-5).

I think it's safe to say that Nebuchadnezzar had a serious issue with anger in his life. If things didn't go his way, he was ready to use his power to hurt someone else. He literally threatened to kill those who were summoned to give him council. And he had the power to follow through with it. He threatened to burn down all their homes—where their families lived. But it didn't stop there.

- Later, when the counselors were unable to know and interpret the king's dream, the Bible tells us, "For this reason the king was angry and very furious, and gave the command to destroy all the wise men of Babylon" (verse 12).
- In another instance, when Daniel's friends disobeyed a decree by Nebuchadnezzar (in obedience to God's laws), the Bible says, "Nebuchadnezzar, in rage and fury, gave the command to bring Shadrach, Meshach, and Abed-Nego. So they brought these men before the king" (3:13).
- And later, "Nebuchadnezzar was full of fury, and the expression on his face changed toward Shadrach, Meshach, and Abed-Nego" (verse 19).

Over time, Nebuchadnezzar's anger progressed, and he was filled with rage and fury.

Anger is destructive. Like a fire, it destroys everything in its path. It destroys people; the very people whom Jesus died for, including the person who is angry. This emotion can be so destructive, so hurtful, that it will forever harm the person it's pointed toward.

And like I mentioned above, anger is an area in a believer's life that's often excused. You've probably heard someone say, "I come from this sort of background or that type of upbringing, so I'm always angry." But that's only an excuse. Or maybe you've heard someone justify their anger by saying, "They deserved it!" Others may claim they exhibited righteous anger. Come on, now. An outburst of wrath isn't righteous. God doesn't want us to justify our anger. He wants us to confess it and forsake it.

There are specific times when anger is appropriate. Yes, there can be righteous anger in you when you recognize sin and evil. But that's not what King Nebuchadnezzar displayed. And that's not what we're talking about in our discussion. Sinful anger is our target. And God forbids sinful anger and enables us with the power of His Spirit to avoid it.

God can deliver you from your anger. I would even put it this way: God *has* delivered you from your anger as a born-again believer in Jesus Christ. And you can walk in the freedom God has given you when you respond to Him by faith and trust Him to do the work. If you let Him, God will replace your anger with the fruit of His Spirit. Then, instead of anger, you'll be filled with love, joy, peace, patience, kindness, goodness, faithfulness, gentleness, and self-control (Galatians 5:22-23).

WORLDLY WISDOM ABOUT ANGER

You can gain wisdom on the topic of anger from the world, or you can get it from the Bible. In this chapter, we will look at both. We will see where the two approaches are alike, and where they differ. First, let's start with how the world views anger.

There are some great suggestions available to us in our world. Professionals will help you with some of the outward things. But worldly wisdom is not the same as God's wisdom. And that is an important distinction to make.

A quick Google search will yield advice of all sorts on how to deal with your anger. Not all of it is bad, actually. I compiled a list of a few of the suggestions and recommendations I found:[3]

1. **Count to ten.** This is a suggestion to count upward to the number ten or downward from ten. You are giving yourself some time to calm down from the issue that angered you.

2. **Take a walk.** By walking around, you are helping to make some space between you and the situation and allowing time to soothe your anger.

3. **Pause and think.** Often, you can avoid saying something you will regret by simply stopping for a few moments and thinking things through. That advice may sound great at first. But unfortunately, when you are in the middle of an anger episode—either someone else's or your own—it's already too late to collect your thoughts. The ability to reason is already lost. Either you, or the other person, are out of control.

4. **Exercise it out.** How about that one? Get some exercise and sweat it out. Physical activity can certainly reduce stress. Personally, I like to sweat things out.

5. **Take a timeout.** "Timeouts aren't just for kids. Give yourself short breaks during times of the day that tend to be stressful. A few moments of quiet time might help you feel better prepared to handle what's ahead without getting irritated or angry."[4] Timeouts can benefit adults just as much as they benefit children. But in the midst of an anger episode, take a timeout? It's good to pause and take a breath, but likely, you won't have the ability to do much more than that. Better to be proactive with this one.

6. **Listen to some music.** I don't know how practical this one is, but if you can do this, make sure you pick the right, soothing songs. Playing the wrong songs could escalate the situation.

7. **Forgive.** This is a huge tool in minimizing your anger. Forgive and release. Number seven aligns with biblical teaching. Don't hold a grudge. This suggestion taps into very good wisdom here. Forgive and release.

8. **Relax.** Tell yourself to take it easy. Can you imagine? Simply say, "Take it easy." This may not work well if you have already responded to a person or situation with your flesh. Nonetheless, it is advice that the world offers.

Worldly wisdom offers some good tips. I'm not minimizing good coping skills. Do whatever it takes—anything short of sin—to bring down your temper a notch. Use tools so you're not flipping out all the time. I recognize it is important. However, if you only listen to advice the world provides on the topic, you'll never deal with the root of the issue.

BIBLICAL WISDOM ABOUT ANGER

The root issue concerning anger is very simple. You're a sinner. It's an embedded bitterness in your heart. Your attempt to control a situation by yelling, screaming, or whatever you're doing is a sin that needs to be confessed and repented of. That's the cause.

The matter is a spiritual one. It's an issue with your heart. And if you neglect the root issue, things won't improve. It's not by might and it's not by power, but it's "'by My Spirit,' says the Lord of hosts" (Zechariah 4:6). It's through God's ability we can address the problem, not our own.

Allow me to establish an argument that there is such a thing as sinful anger. The Bible says,

> Understand this, my dear brothers and sisters: You must all be quick to listen, slow to speak, and slow to get angry.

> Human anger does not produce the righteousness God desires (James 1:19-20 NLT).

Listen to the Bible. Your anger can never make things right in God's sight. Accept that by faith. That's what God teaches us in His Word. He is the One who created us. He knows us best. As the New King James Version puts it, "The wrath of man does not produce the righteousness of God" (James 1:20).

Anger never makes anything right—never. This is an important principle to hold on to. The wrath of man is not going to take you where you want to go.

But in the Spirit—when you submit to Him—God can temper your temper. Jesus can strengthen you and teach you how to lower it, step by step. You won't get there by repeating little words and phrases. Rather, Jesus will literally remove the root of anger from your heart and enable you to forgive.

Proverbs 29:11 says, "A fool vents all his feelings, but a wise man holds them back." It's not okay to blow up. It's simply not okay. Famously, a young lady once spoke to the great evangelist Billy Sunday after he delivered a strong, stirring message on the topic of anger. She was trying to rationalize, justify, and explain away her anger. So, after the service, she told the pastor, "There's nothing wrong with losing my temper. I blow up, and then it's all over." To which the pastor replied, "So does a shotgun, and look at the damage that it leaves behind."[5]

It's true. Anger always leaves damage. And often, it leaves long-term damage.

Anger is a universal issue. It affects those who follow God and those who don't. Earlier, we looked at an example from someone who wasn't following God, Nebuchadnezzar. Now, let's look at an example of someone who did follow God. You may be surprised by who.

His name is Moses.

Anger is a devastating emotion. And we see it present throughout Moses' life. He never dealt with his anger, and it cost him greatly. Even mighty men of God can make serious mistakes.

I've seen the same thing play out today, when someone doesn't deal with their anger. You have an outburst, and you get on with life. Then, you have another outburst, and you get on with life. You might think, *It's not a big deal. After all, my family is still together. I haven't lost my job over it.* But it is a big deal. Every. Single. Time.

Don't confuse God's patience with His approval. Don't confuse the mercy of people around you by concluding that they didn't get hurt by what you said or did.

Let's look at scenarios from the virtual world. The email you sent was harsh, and you shouldn't have sent it. You should've stopped and prayed, instead of reacted. You know what you posted on social media was harmful, justifying it by stating that it's simply your opinion. But the post hurt people and made others stumble. And it's possible that you're not aware of the consequences of your anger because you had been in such a state of rage that you don't even remember what happened.

You must deal with your anger. If you don't, you could miss out on the promises of God. Of course, you are still a believer if you've put your faith in Christ, but you won't fully receive all that God has for you. You'll be stuck until you're willing to confess and forsake the sin of anger.

For Moses, it started while he was a young man. In Exodus 2, we read he murdered someone. He thought he was doing something good for God. When he saw an Egyptian beating a fellow Hebrew, he went over and killed the Egyptian. It quickly became known that Moses did this, and because of it, he spent the next 40 years in the desert.

Did you know that murder is tied to anger? God's Word tells us it is. Many Christians live their lives thinking they're doing okay because they've never murdered anyone. But we must listen to Jesus' words very carefully. When He taught on issues of the heart, Jesus said,

> You have heard that it was said to those of old, "You shall not murder, and whoever murders will be in danger of the judgment." But I say to you that whoever is angry with his brother without a cause shall be in danger of the judgment (Matthew 5:21-22).

If anger toward someone resides in your heart, it carries the same weight as if you've murdered them in your heart. Often, we are more guilty of sin than we're willing to admit. If we come to Jesus Christ and allow Him to teach us and lead us, He has freedom waiting for us.

After Moses lived in the desert for 40 years, God brought him back. Moses started obeying God. He got to see God. He got to hear from God. Moses stood up to Pharaoh and he led the children of Israel out of slavery. Those are amazing things. God was doing a great work in Moses' life.

The Bible describes Moses as "very humble, more than all men who were on the face of the earth" (Numbers 12:3). Most of the time, he was faithful, sensitive, obedient, and self-sacrificial. But he also had an area inside himself that he never dealt with. There was an ongoing struggle throughout his life. Moses would sin in anger, then conversely, he'd be obedient.

We see Moses' anger rise again in Exodus 16. While the Israelites were in the wilderness, God provided miraculous bread from heaven for them to eat called manna. On the first occasion of this miracle, Moses gave the Israelites God's instruction to only gather enough manna for each person in each tent for one day. Moses told them not to keep any of it until morning (Exodus 16:16-19).

> But some of them didn't listen and kept some of it until morning. But by then it was full of maggots and had a terrible smell. Moses was very angry with them (Exodus 16:20 NLT).

It says that Moses was *very angry* with them. We are not told what Moses' actions were, only that he had a flare up of anger, and then, he returned to a life of obedience.

Later, we read about another episode of Moses' anger. This occurrence was sparked when the Israelites built a golden calf to worship, while Moses was away receiving God's covenant on Mount Sinai. This time, the Bible says that Moses "burned with anger" (Exodus 32:19 NLT). When Moses came down the mountain, he threw down the stone tablets with God's covenant written on them, smashing them to pieces.

Moses' anger was progressive. And it would be the last episode of his life that would hold him back.

A PARENT'S ANGER IS DESTRUCTIVE

Before we discuss Moses' final anger episode, I want to speak to parents who struggle with anger. Please hear me. Sinful anger is destructive to your children. Some of you are self-deceived into thinking that your anger is helping you raise righteous and godly kids who will love God with all their hearts, soul, and mind. It's not. It is accomplishing the exact opposite. Your out-of-control anger is damaging your kids.

I understand that some may have been raised by an angry parent or grandparent. So maybe, you think that's just how life is. That's how your grandfather was, that's how your dad was, and that's just how you are. They were okay, so you'll be okay too. But likely, if you carefully examine your dad and your grandpa, you'll find that they didn't make out as well as what appeared on the surface. Their own parents' anger deeply wounded them. And it hurt them. That's why they became angry. And the anger was then handed down from each person—mom or dad.

I know this from experience. I grew up in a very angry home. My parents were very loving and wonderful. But one of my parents chose to parent in an angry way. I'll admit that I was a challenging and difficult kid. But challenging and difficult kids don't deserve angry parents.

I assure you that I'm okay now. My parent and I settled this issue a long time ago, and there's been forgiveness. They did the best they could with what they had. God was gracious and merciful to us. And all is well. They are in heaven right now rejoicing.

Although it's not unusual for people to have an anger streak because of how they were raised, I don't want you to think it is justification for angry parenting yourself. I want you to understand what happens when you run your house with anger. There are four things that happen when your kids live in an angry home.

1. You get compliance.

First, when you're angry and out of control with your kids, you're going to get compliance. They will do what you tell them to do. But don't confuse their compliance with godly obedience. Generally, that's not what they are doing. Your kids aren't necessarily complying with the Lord.

Instead, they're frightened and they want you to stop acting in anger. They're smart enough to know what's going on. They're scared, and they will do whatever it takes for you to stop and calm down.

2. Your kids begin to harden their hearts.

When you're angry with your kids, the second thing that happens is they begin to harden their hearts. They're hardening their hearts toward you. It's very difficult to follow a person who is angry. Anger breaks the line of trust. It's hard to trust someone that you're scared of.

Your kids aren't going to tell you this because they're afraid of you. And when children are small, they don't understand. They're only beginning to develop their thinking. They don't know how to deduce that something is massively wrong in their house. They don't know how to talk to their parents about it. They are only kids.

3. Your kids become fearful.

The third thing that happens in an angry home is your kids become fearful. This builds from the second point—I want you to understand the size difference between you and your young kids.

You are bigger than your kids. You're stronger than they are. You're more capable of doing things. Your physical presence looms large for them. It can be difficult for adults to place themselves in their children's shoes. We don't look at things from a child's perspective anymore. A large angry presence is frightening to them.

When you fly off the handle, your kids are physically scared. And they shut down and harden their hearts toward you. You may think they're being obedient, but they're simply scared.

4. Your kids learn to avoid you.

The fourth thing that happens with your kids is something I call avoidance. We as Christian parents all want the same thing for our kids. We want them to love God and serve Him with all their heart, soul, and mind. And we want to enjoy time with our kids all the way to eternity. We want them to be a part of our lives.

But if your children grow up in an angry home, they will learn to avoid you at a young age. The less they face your anger, the better. So they will choose to avoid you. And if that never gets resolved, they will continue to avoid you as adults. They simply won't want to deal with it.

When drugs, alcohol, and drunkenness are mixed in to that environment, it's a disaster. And yes, I'm still talking about Christian homes. In the homes of those who say they are following God.

If you have never noticed these things, God wants to reveal them to you. Your kids are precious in the sight of the Lord. And I know that you love them. It's never too late to get back on track. You can still express love to your kids and mend the relationship.

Before I was saved, anger had a predominant presence in my life.

That was partly because of the kind of home I grew up in, but it was also because I chose to live that way. It was my responsibility. As I grew older, I entered a serious relationship with my wife and that's how I treated her. When we had our son, that's how I treated him. I began raising my son by yelling at him. My home was an angry home.

But then, I got saved. I was born again. And God delivered me from that root of anger. God began a sanctifying work in me. God replaced my thinking rooted in anger with the right kind of thinking. God taught me to love my wife and my kids and serve them. I learned to encourage, disciple, and train my children.

Now, no parent is perfect. Don't expect perfection from yourself. God meets us where we're at in His grace. But I'm going to share with you a tool that will stop the madness. God gave it to me, and it will do a work in you and your kids. Of all the tools God gave me as a parent, this has been, by far, the most important one. It's been one of the most effective. It's something I never saw or heard in practice while growing up.

Learn how to get down on your knees, where you're at eye level with your kids. Then, look your kids in the eye and say, "Will you forgive me? I was wrong, and I sinned against you in my anger." And ask your kids, "Will you pray for me?"

I'm telling you, it's one of the most powerful, God-honoring things that you can do in your life. And it's never too late.

Your little kiddos will grow up. But you can still do this no matter their age. It opens the floodgates, which leads to forgiveness. It opens the door for God to do a work of reconciliation between you and your kids. And you will be free.

There are a number of studies that show the high numbers of kids who leave the church after high school. Once those kids grow up, they're not walking with God anymore. I'm going to suggest to you that many kids who lived in angry homes stopped walking with God earlier than that. They went to Sunday school and learned about a merciful, loving God. And then, boom, they went right back in their homes that were filled with anger.

It's devastating. I realize there are multiple reasons why kids aren't following the Lord later in life. But for many of them, they didn't live in a home that honored God. In their home, anger was the predominant emotion. And now, they equate God with anger. God wants to release both parents and children from this.

THE LAST EPISODE OF ANGER IN MOSES' LIFE

Let's return to Moses. We find the last episode of anger in Moses' life in Numbers 20. At the time, the children of Israel are still wandering in the wilderness, relying on the provision of God. After Moses' previous outbursts of anger, God was gracious. But in his last one, Moses went too far.

The major episodes of anger in your life will include you taking things too far. I promise you. Often, a reason people come to speak with a pastor one-on-one is because of their last major episode of anger. It can happen when

- *you find yourself in the back of a police car.*
- *you end up getting drunk in a bar and hurting someone.*
- *your wife finally walks out on you and files divorce papers.*
- *your kids rebel.*
- *you lose your job.*

But it doesn't need to happen that way.

You see, the last episode of your anger in your life could be met with repentance. You don't need to take things that far. To be clear, I'm not talking about times when you get frustrated. We all get frustrated sometimes. I'm talking about ongoing outbursts of wrath and sinful anger that surround your life. And the last one you'll regret, unless you repent before you go that far.

Let's look at what happened in the life of Moses.

> The LORD spoke to Moses, saying, "Take the rod; you and your brother Aaron gather the congregation together. Speak to the rock before their eyes" (Numbers 20:7-8).

God told Moses to speak to the rock. How do we speak? With our mouths. It's very straightforward. If you were Moses, you would understand what God asked you to do. Speak to the rock. Pretty easy. I know it's elementary. But sometimes we need to make it super simple. Otherwise, we take what God's Word says and twist it. And that's when we get in trouble.

So God told Moses to speak to the rock and He told Moses what would happen. God said,

> It will yield its water; thus you shall bring water for them out of the rock, and give drink to the congregation and their animals (verse 8).

We learn something about God here. He wants to quench the thirst of the children of Israel. He wants to bless them. He wants to take care of them. And He wants to use Moses to do it. God wants to give the Israelites the water they need for themselves and their animals. God loves them.

Now, Moses had dealt with years of rebellion from the people. Many times, the people showed contempt for Moses' leadership and expressed their wishes to return to slavery in Egypt. He experienced years of difficulty as he led Israel. Yet, what was God's perspective? God loved them. He desired to give them water and He told Moses how Moses was to go about providing it. It was going to be a great miracle. Go to the rock, talk to it, and everyone will have their needs met.

And what did Moses do?

> Moses took the rod from before the LORD as He commanded him. And Moses and Aaron gathered the assembly together before the rock; and he said to *them* (verses 9-10, emphasis added).

Whoa, wait a minute. What did God say? He told Moses to speak to the rock. What did Moses do? He spoke to the assembly of Israel.

We've all made that mistake before. God gives you a crystal-clear command. And along the way in following through with your responsibilities in it, you change it.

Why did Moses change his task? Because he was angry. The truth of God gets distorted when we live in the flesh. Moses was an angry man. And instead of speaking to the rock, he spoke to the people. And Moses said,

> Hear now, you rebels! Must we bring water for you out of this rock? (verse 10).

And it doesn't end there. It gets worse. Moses took his rod, and he struck the rock. The Bible tells us,

> Moses lifted his hand and struck the rock twice with his rod; and water came out abundantly, and the congregation and their animals drank (verse 11).

Moses disobeyed God's command in more than one way. He spoke to the people. He expressed his anger with them. Then, he hit the rock and water came out.

Moses could have rationalized his disobedience to God. And maybe at first, you would come to the same conclusion. He might have decided that he followed God's command the right way because water came out of the rock. Maybe he thought, *I know God told me to speak to the rock, and I did it my way. Water still came out. So it's okay. Everything is fine. I got what I wanted and the people got what they wanted.*

But that's not how God views our disobedience. Our disobedience is strictly disobedience in the eyes of God. It's sinful. When God tells you to speak to the rock, speak to it. And don't strike it at all.

And we need to notice what Moses wasn't aware of. Often, God will tell us to do something and we won't know why He asked us to do it the way that He commanded. God is at work in your life right now. But you don't know the full reason a situation or circumstance is present in your life. You don't know why He gave you a certain instruction in a particular way. You can't see all the things that are occurring behind the scenes. You simply don't know. But the fact that we don't know is no excuse to be disobedient.

Moses didn't know that the rock was a picture and a type of Jesus Christ. In the New Testament, we read,

> They drank of that spiritual Rock that followed them, and that Rock was Christ (1 Corinthians 10:4).

God used that rock giving forth water as a picture. Years later, Jesus stood on the teaching steps leading into the Temple and He said,

> If anyone thirsts, let him come to Me and drink. He who believes in Me, as the Scripture has said, out of his heart will flow rivers of living water (John 7:37-38).

The rock was a picture of Jesus. And when Jesus was struck, He was struck once, not twice.

We can see here, you can get clear direction from God and totally mess it up. Yet God will still accomplish what He wants to do. But don't believe God is pleased by your disobedience. Just because God still follows through with what He said He would do, it doesn't mean He's pleased with you doing your part your own way.

And God wasn't pleased with Moses either. The book of Numbers tells us, "Then the LORD spoke to Moses and Aaron, 'Because you did not believe Me…'" (20:12).

Pause there for a second. Where in the text leading up to this does it say that Moses didn't believe God? It doesn't. God looked at Moses' life and concluded: Your anger made you an unbeliever. Anger is a form of unbelief.

So God told Moses and Aaron,

> Because you did not believe Me, to hallow Me in the eyes of the children of Israel, therefore you shall not bring this assembly into the land which I have given them (verse 12).

Now, many times, I've been taught that Moses didn't honor the Lord. That's true. And now you understand *why* he didn't represent God properly. It was his anger and his disobedience. There were moments when Moses twisted the Word of God. He didn't completely obey. God loved His people even in their rebellion, in the same way He loves you and me. But when we don't completely obey God, there will be consequences. Moses' disobedience in anger is why he was not allowed to enter the promised land, even after years of leading God's people.

THE FIVE ESSENTIALS OF RIGHTEOUS ANGER

If you still believe your anger is okay, here are five things you should ask yourself when you start to justify your anger. If *all* five are present at the same time, then it's okay to be angry.

1. You're angry, and you do not sin (Ephesians 4:26).
2. You're angry, and you don't go to sleep with it present or lingering. "Do not let the sun go down on your wrath" (Ephesians 4:26).
3. Your anger is from God—not from your own selfishness and desire to control, which are works of the flesh (Galatians 5:19-20).
4. Your anger achieves the righteousness of God. "For the wrath of man does not produce the righteousness of God" (James 1:20).
5. Your anger comes slowly (Proverbs 16:32).

If you possess all five of those things, then you may proceed carefully and safely in your anger. Rarely do all of these occur at the same time in our lives. Anger is usually a control mechanism. A lot of our anger comes from annoyances. And anger, unforgiveness, and bitterness are all cousins.

SINFUL ANGER IS A HEART ISSUE

Sinful anger is not from the Lord for any of us. As the Bible tells us, *now* is the time to get rid of anger (Colossians 3:8). Also, "An angry person starts fights" (Proverbs 29:22 NLT).

Anger is a heart issue. Jesus said,

> A good tree can't produce bad fruit, and a bad tree can't produce good fruit. A tree is identified by its fruit. Figs are never gathered from thornbushes, and grapes are not picked from bramble bushes. A good person produces good things from the treasury of a good heart, and an evil person produces evil things from the treasury of an

> evil heart. *What you say flows from what is in your heart* (Luke 6:43-45 NLT, emphasis added).

Or as the New King James Version translates the final sentence of verse 45, "For out of the abundance of the heart his mouth speaks."

Jesus clearly teaches us that anger is a heart issue. That's it. The problem with your anger is a problem of your heart. And because we don't know our own hearts, the Bible exhorts us to ask God to reveal what is in them. Like the psalmist, you can say,

> Search me, O God, and know my heart; test me and know my anxious thoughts. Point out anything in me that offends you, and lead me along the path of everlasting life (Psalm 139:23-24 NLT).

Ask God to reveal any hidden sin in you. Ask Him to show you what offends you and hurts others. After He reveals it, follow the words of 1 John 1:9, "If we confess our sins, He is faithful and just to forgive us our sins and to cleanse us from all unrighteousness."

Don't simply feel bad about your anger once it is revealed to you. Confess it. Repent of it as the sin that it is. And let God start to do a cleansing work in your heart.

As you allow God to do work in your heart, begin filling your heart and mind with the things that the Bible tells us we are to think about. Fix your thoughts on things that are true, noble, just, pure, lovely, and of good report. Think about things that are virtuous and praiseworthy (Philippians 4:8).

If you meditate on good things, the abundance of your heart will be filled with the grace of God and His mercy. He will give you that grace and mercy because He loves you. And while you're still alive, it's never too late to get right with God.

Moses never entered the promised land. Or did he? A careful

reading of the Scriptures tells us that Moses didn't get there with his own generation. He died in the land of Moab, outside the promised land (Deuteronomy 34:1-5). But later, by God's grace, Moses did spend some time in the promised land. That's how much God loved Moses. Remember when Jesus was up on the Mount of Transfiguration? While He was there, He was met by two people who were fully alive (Matthew 17:1-3). Their names? Elijah and Moses. You bet he got in. God is so good to us.

God loves you too. He's gracious, caring, and compassionate. And He wants what's best for you and your family. God doesn't forbid sin only because it stands against His holiness and His glory, although that is a serious thing. God forbids sin in our lives because it destroys us. Any good father wants to protect his children from the things that will destroy them.

I am a living example that God can change someone's life. Before my oldest son passed away, we settled all the strife that happened between us when he was young. He was so forgiving and loving. After this forgiveness, my other children were born into a godly home. They weren't born to perfect parents, but they were born to growing parents in a process of sanctification. Parents who worked out their differences, humbled themselves, asked each other for forgiveness, and let the Spirit of God work through their weaknesses.

That is God's will for your family too. He wants to work in your family by His Spirit.

I want to share with you some final thoughts from God's Word that drive home the point that anger is a big deal. Following are a few verses from Proverbs and Psalms that talk about anger.

- "A fool is quick-tempered, but a wise person stays calm when insulted" (Proverbs 12:16 NLT).
- "Short-tempered people do foolish things, and schemers are hated" (Proverbs 14:17 NLT).

- "People with understanding control their anger; a hot temper shows great foolishness" (Proverbs 14:29 NLT).
- "A hot-tempered person starts fights; a cool-tempered person stops them" (Proverbs 15:18 NLT).
- "Better to be patient than powerful; better to have self-control than to conquer a city" (Proverbs 16:32 NLT).
- "Sensible people control their temper; they earn respect by overlooking wrongs" (Proverbs 19:11 NLT).
- "Fools vent their anger, but the wise quietly hold it back" (Proverbs 29:11 NLT).
- "Stop being angry! Turn from your rage! Do not lose your temper—it only leads to harm" (Psalm 37:8 NLT).

The Bible has a lot to say about sinful anger. Sinful anger hurts others. And sinful anger hurts you.

Reckoning with the Bible on this issue requires a response. If you have a problem with anger, you need to confess that sin. Pray to God and admit that you have a problem with anger. Agree with God that your anger is a sin. Tell God that now you want to do things His way. Cry it out. Let God wash you with the tears you shed. Every single tear you shed is kept in a bottle by God (Psalm 56:8). Allow God to cleanse you.

You can't change the past. But you can change the future. And that's God's will for you. He wants the very best for you. He wants you to be alive and filled with His Spirit. He doesn't want you hiding sin. And He doesn't want you to be a victim of abuse or the one giving abuse. He wants cleanliness and purity. And He's doing the work. You just need to meet Him there.

REFLECTION/DISCUSSION QUESTIONS

1. Is there business that you need to do with the Lord regarding your sinful anger? If so, do that now.
2. How have you seen anger shape interactions with you or in your home?
3. Is there someone who you need to ask for forgiveness? Do it today!
4. Anger, unforgiveness, and bitterness are all related. How have you found that to be true in your life? Think about a time when one led to another. How did the Lord help you to break the cycle?

7

DEALING WITH THE PRESENT

At this point, we've discussed many biblical truths that will help you to let go of your past. But now, I want to show you where you get the power to put those biblical truths into practice. You will find that power day by day and moment by moment in Jesus. You must abide in Him.

In John 15, God gives us the beautiful picture of the vine and the vinedresser. Jesus said,

> I am the true vine, and My Father is the vinedresser. Every branch in Me that does not bear fruit He takes away; and every branch that bears fruit He prunes, that it may bear more fruit. You are already clean because of the word which I have spoken to you. Abide in Me, and I in you. As the branch cannot bear fruit of itself, unless it abides in the vine, neither can you, unless you abide in Me. I am the vine, you are the branches. He who abides in Me, and I in him, bears much fruit; for without Me you can do nothing (verses 1-5).

In this passage, Jesus brings us back to what's very important in our relationship with Him. It's not religious expression. It is not our religious heritage. It's not the activities that we do. The thing we need to learn how to do in our relationship with Him is to abide.

Relationship paints a beautiful picture. We all have relationships at the human level. We know that relationships grow over time. They grow with time and testing. They are not a formality.

If following Jesus was simply a bunch of outward activities, many Christians would be very good followers because we know how to do outward tasks well. But our relationship with Jesus is not about the outward appearance. It's about our inside.

In these verses in John, we learn just how well the vinedresser takes care of us. That's where the emphasis is. The vinedresser cultivates the vineyard and tends the vine. The vinedresser is a picture of God the Father, the true vine is a picture of Jesus, and the branches are a picture of born-again believers.

God the Father, as the vinedresser, is the One who cares for us. And as born-again believers, we need to be connected to the true vine, Jesus, if we want to grow and be fruitful. We receive all our spiritual nourishment through our connection to Him.

There are many people who love to garden. When spring comes, it's gardening time. Gardeners care for the plants they grow in a wonderful way. Doing it well takes time, dedication, and study. For each plant, gardeners determine ideal conditions for the healthy growth of their plants, such as the right soil, light, and watering plan.

Imagine how much more God the Father cares for you. Think about how much and the many ways in which He takes care of you. Like He did with the nation of Israel, God is still looking for fruit among His church.

The good news is that our fruit—like the fruit on a tree or the grapes on a vine—occurs naturally. It develops through our relationship with God.

Many of us don't think too much about it. And some of us don't take the time to care. But when you see fruit or a flower, it is a powerful reminder of what happens through a relationship with the Lord.

There's no need for a tree to work hard in its effort to produce fruit. For instance, you don't hear a tree groaning as you walk by it. Trees aren't making faces marked with exertion. They're not stressing out because their job is to produce fruit. That's not how it works. Instead, when a tree is planted in the right area by a caring farmer and it is given water and proper nutrients, it grows; and its fruit comes naturally.

Why the long discussion about fruit? The truth is that you're in the best place you can be as a believer as you abide in Christ and produce fruit. Think of it this way, the production of fruit in your life is the natural outcome of God's presence in your life. So if there's no fruit from your life, it shows that you're not abiding.

When you're not abiding, the Bible identifies that as being in your flesh. In your flesh, you rely on your own resources, which are all empty. In relation to our topic, you will lack the power you need to move forward from your past if you're not abiding in Christ.

The Bible describes the fruit that is produced in your life as a result of abiding in Jesus. This fruit will occur naturally in your life as you abide in Him:

- winning souls (Romans 1:13)
- holiness (Romans 6:22)
- giving financially (Romans 15:28)
- helping others practically (Colossians 1:6)
- giving praise to God (Hebrews 13:15)
- love (Galatians 5:22)

Also, there are fruit of the Spirit listed in Galatians. Some believe they are all a manifestation of one fruit of the Spirit—love. Others view them as separate fruit. I think it could be interpreted either way. In addition to love, the fruit of the Spirit is joy, peace, patience, kindness, goodness, faithfulness, gentleness, and self-control (Galatians 5:22-23).

Recall, the key to bearing fruit is the word *abide*. Why is abiding so important? Abiding is necessary because Jesus tells us, "Without Me, you can do nothing" (John 15:5).

It's very important for us to fully understand that truth. As we walk with Jesus Christ and serve Him, we can't do anything without Him. That goes for all of us. As I exercise the gift of pastor-teacher and as I have the privilege of leading and serving, I must remember that without Jesus, I can do nothing.

We must recognize, we can do a lot of things without Jesus. We can produce things. We can engage in religious activities. We can be very active and busy. We can even do things using Jesus' name, but without Jesus. However, I'm telling you this: Without Jesus, you can do nothing of eternal value. You can't do anything that reflects His love and His character.

Jesus can take a person from producing no fruit to producing much fruit by His indwelling presence. The key is to abide. It's the difference between walking in the flesh and walking in the Spirit. Or the contrast between living under the Old Covenant and living under the New Covenant.

Jesus has invaded our lives. Later in John 15, it says,

> You did not choose Me, but I chose you and appointed you that you should go and bear fruit, and that your fruit should remain, that whatever you ask the Father in My name He may give you (verse 16).

There's a lot of talk today about how we choose Jesus—our choice to follow and respond to the gospel. In one sense, I understand using that kind of language. But the reality is that Jesus chose you. Jesus sought you out. He wanted to enter a relationship with you. And

He wants to take over, so you will become more and more like Him. If you really want to start growing and bearing much fruit, then you must let Jesus rearrange your life.

The life of a disciple of Jesus is a life reordered. Jesus accepts you as you are and He loves you as you are. But He doesn't let you stay that way. Your entire life is a process of Jesus conforming you into His image. The Bible refers to this process as sanctification.

Recently, I was meditating on Romans 12:2. That verse speaks of not being conformed to this world. As the J.B. Phillips New Testament puts it, "Don't let the world around you squeeze you into its own mould." I like that picture because it is effective. Whatever gets pressed into a mold matches the mold's form.

You have likely noticed that the world system we live under has a distinct form. It possesses an ideal. Although it shifts and changes, the root of that form is godlessness. It's a world without God and without accountability. It's a world where people operate much like people did during the leadership of Israel's judges—where everyone does what is right in their own eyes. There's a general emptiness in the world. And those who are separated from Jesus are spending their entire lives trying to fill that emptiness.

Often, the people in the world who have the most money and the greatest notoriety tend to be some of the most miserable. It seems that every day the news shares another story about a celebrity who goes to rehab, checks in for mental health treatment, or even takes their own life. They're unable to cope.

Unfortunately, that's not only a worldly struggle. Many believers have a hard time coping with the difficulties of life. When a challenge presents itself in your life, you have a choice to make. You can abide in Christ—the perfect place of peace. Or, you can follow the ways of the world and choose to rely on coping mechanisms that amount to idolatry. The worldly options may give you temporary peace, but they will not give you any permanent, eternal help.

The solution to life's problems is to abide—to live moment by moment in dependence on Jesus Christ. Moment...by...moment.

When Jesus taught His disciples to pray, He told them to ask God for their daily bread (Matthew 6:11). When was the last time that daily bread was of great concern to you? I know that even in a world of great excess, there are those who struggle. And we have other needs as well. I know some who have difficulties with paying their rent. Not long ago, someone asked me for prayer because he needed $1,000 for his rent. His face showed great concern. He had an emergency come up, so he used his rent money to take care of that. I laid hands on him and we prayed together. He left our time together filled with peace and hope because we had sought the Lord. Well, wouldn't you know it? The day before his rent was due, the funds he needed showed up. He received his tax refund. And this circumstance serves as a testimony to God's provision.

Whether it's your daily bread or a mortgage payment, Jesus taught us that we need to live a life of dependence on Him, moment by moment. And if we can learn how to reduce our lives down to moment-by-moment dependence on Jesus, we will receive peace from Him—moment by moment.

We need to obey God. He told us to cast our cares on Him because He cares for us (1 Peter 5:7). When you're relying on Jesus moment by moment, that's when you're abiding in Him.

The word *abide* in John 15:4 comes from the Greek word *meno*. And it simply means to remain; to dwell; to stay put.[1] It speaks of intimacy, closeness, and a permanent attachment.

I like how the Message paraphrase renders the verse:

> Live in me. Make your home in me just as I do in you. In the same way that a branch can't bear grapes by itself but only by being joined to the vine, you can't bear fruit unless you are joined with me (John 15:4 MSG).

I like that phrase, "Make your home in me." That is a great picture.

Consider this, when you're on your way home from being away, your goal is not to get close to your house. You don't arrive at the street you live on and walk into any house on the block. No, you have a habit. And it's a good habit. You go to *your* house. You go to the place God gave you to dwell in. That place is your refuge. It's where you rest, sleep, eat, and enjoy family and friends. It's your home.

Just as you do with your physical home, make your spiritual home in Jesus. Make it in *Him*.

The New Living Translation says, "Yes, I am the vine; you are the branches. Those who remain in me, and I in them, will produce much fruit. For apart from me you can do nothing" (John 15:5 NLT).

Here is the key. The way to deal with your past—with the issues that inflame your emotions and the great hurt that you've endured from the consequences of your own bad decisions or someone else's—is to remain in Christ. Because the alternative is to run around, carelessly and aimlessly. Before we were saved, we wandered. There was no purpose or goal to our pursuits. We were living life in any way that we wanted. We invested in activities that gave us a false sense of good based on our own definition. But that sort of life does not bear fruit. We only find strength and produce fruit when we abide in Jesus, when we remain and stay put in His presence.

So how do you do that? What happens when you abide in Jesus? It's not by following some esoteric, spiritual teaching where you sit on your couch without moving. It is much different than that.

AN ATTITUDE OF BELIEF

First, abiding begins with a confession of faith. It's a confession that you trust Jesus and His sufficiency in your life. It involves knowing the Word of God and speaking the truth into your life.

For example, do you have a burden today? If you do, confess the scripture that tells you to cast all your cares upon God because He cares for you (1 Peter 5:7). Tell yourself, *I'm going to cast my cares upon You today, God.* When you do this, you make a statement of abiding. You are saying to the Lord, *I'm not going to run to a coping mechanism that I've established as an idol. I'm not going to get worked up by the issue. I'm not going to get mad about it. Instead, I am going to cast my care upon You today, God, because that's what You said to do and You will take care of it.* You can do this before the Lord in your prayer time.

It begins with a confession, a statement of agreement with God's Word. Of course, God's Word is true whether you confess it—whether you agree with it—or not. It always stands true. But for God's Word to bring change to your life, you need to apply it. You say, *Lord, I'm going to cast this care upon You today.*

Second, abiding is done with a steady obedience. In John 14:15, Jesus declared, "If you love Me, keep My commandments." Jesus said *if* you love Him. If Jesus came to you today and asked, "I've got a quick question for you: Do you love Me?" what would you say in reply? I hope you would answer, "Yes, of course."

When you say yes, Jesus will respond, "Keep My commandments." His commandments are not burdensome (1 John 5:3). His yoke is easy, and His burden is light (Matthew 11:30). Keep His commandments. That's at the root of abiding—obedience.

Think about it. As you're saying, *Father, I come to You in prayer*, you're in a place of obedience. As you start speaking forth the Word that is ministering to you, you're in obedience. Your mind is focused. Your lips are following. And your actions will follow that. It starts with a confession. And it's followed up through obedience.

The *how* of abiding doesn't begin with a task. It's not a work that gets you there but an attitude. It's by an attitude of believing what God has said.

This is not a practice that is unfamiliar to us. We already live with an attitude of belief in other things. Back to our house example, when you're out somewhere and you're ready to go home, you travel back home and walk into your house without even thinking about it. You simply begin by heading in that direction. You don't need to consult a map. You're confident. You know where you live. The journey home is so common to you that you don't need to walk yourself through the steps. You don't get in your car and tell yourself, *I'm going to go home. I live at 123 Main Street, and I'm going to get there in 15 minutes.* You don't do that. You have done it so many times that it's very natural for you. And your attitude—your belief—is that you're going to successfully navigate to your home.

When it comes to our relationship with Jesus Christ, it's the same. When your mind is stirring and you can't control it—when your thoughts and feelings are overwhelming you—you can tell yourself, *I'm going to go home spiritually. I'm overwhelmed by my thoughts, Lord. And I'm coming home.*

The how in abiding begins with an attitude of going home. And it's followed by an attitude of dependence on Jesus. That requires humility. You need to admit that you can't produce any fruit on your own.

Sometimes when we are faced with difficulties, it seems like we need to hurry to gather our thoughts and react. But we are unable to gather our thoughts spiritually without the power of the Holy Spirit. It starts with Jesus. Jesus doesn't show up in the middle. We need to begin our response to our challenges with Him. When we gather our thoughts and react apart from Christ, those problems are going to come back larger and harder to work through. That's the reality of living in this broken world.

How does this relate to the past? The past is a great accuser, especially concerning the things we regret, the circumstances we wish had never happened, and the situations we would avoid if we had another chance. Yet who you are now is based on everything you did in your past. As we've learned, the Bible says, "There is therefore now no condemnation to those who are in Christ Jesus" (Romans 8:1). What is another way of describing being "in Christ"? Abiding. The Bible is one message. It is all about getting us to Jesus. Jesus took care of all our sin by taking our punishment on Himself. Because of what He did, we have a refuge in God.

When the Bible talks about God being our refuge, it speaks of abiding. Proverbs 18:10 says, "The name of the LORD is a strong tower; the righteous run to it and are safe." That verse speaks of abiding.

We can be guilty of reading this verse and believing that we have a part to play, or an action to take. You may think to yourself, *The name of the Lord is a strong tower. But the tower is way over there, and I don't have the energy to run way over there.* This verse has nothing to do with what we do; rather, it is a picture of trusting God. Simply change your mind. It's not about you and your works. It's a mindset. And it starts with an attitude of belief.

AN ATTITUDE OF DEPENDENCE

You know yourself. And you can recognize if you are taking on an attitude of dependence. Do you depend on God or do you depend on your own strength? One of the greatest barriers to an attitude of dependence on God is pride. When you've failed with your pride, you can't be dependent on Him until you acknowledge your failure, receive God's forgiveness, and abide in Him again. Put aside your pride.

The person who is the most disappointed in your failures is you. We can get so disappointed in ourselves. We kick ourselves and we replay the failure in our minds and tell ourselves, *I wish I'd never done that.* There are things in my life now that are consequences of actions I took years ago. And believe me, I wish I hadn't done them. Let me share one instance that illustrates the importance of depending on God rather than depending on ourselves.

One of the practices I encourage the men and women who serve in our church to apply is not to use email for difficult conversations.

I find myself using email less and less. A sentence or two in an email is all I'll write. And even then, the potential always exists that I can mess up a relationship in only a sentence or two.

Soon after the passing of my son, I received a difficult email. When I opened it, I couldn't believe my eyes. I thought, *What is this? I can't believe this. I can't believe that this person believes what they wrote about me and my family.*

What did I do in response? Did I take that email before the Lord like King Hezekiah took his letter from Sennacherib (Isaiah 37:14)? Did I ask, *God, what would You like me to do, my great defender, with this email?*

No. I sat down in my home office, opened my laptop, and began to answer that email—point by point. It was a very difficult time for me and tensions were very high. My other son had recently come back from Bible college. He walked by my office and said, "Dad, don't do that. Don't write the email. You know you're not supposed to use email like that. We should pray." And I replied, "No, no, that was for you. I'm the exception," or some dumb response like that. The trouble was I was serious.

My wife was in the kitchen and said, "Don't write that email!" My reply: "No."

After I wrote my retort, I sent it to my wife and asked her to read it. I don't remember exactly how our conversation went. But no one approved of me sending that email, including God.

Yet, I remember hitting the send button. And after you do that, you can't take it back. I remember how self-justified I felt. I anticipated how that email would vindicate my family and the situation. However, it did none of those things. It only emboldened the enemy to stir up more strife and more difficulty. To this day, fallout from that email remains part of some of the difficulties we face as a family. The reach of the consequences is unbelievable.

We all have things we regret. If I had the chance to go back, I would have never sent the reply that I did. And I'm sharing this with you, so you don't commit the same failure that I did. Instead, take the offense to God like Hezekiah did (2 Kings 19:14-19). Lay it before the Lord and let Him take care of it.

A principle I learned from pastor Chuck Smith is you have two choices when it comes to defending yourself. The first choice is to go ahead and defend yourself. You have the freedom to do that. And God will allow you to do so. But with what resources? An email? A few choice words? An argument? You'll be limited by your own resources.

Or you can choose the second option. By faith, you can let God defend you. In both the Old and New Testaments, we see examples of people who abided in God and allowed Him to do the work. When you allow God to be your defense, you're depending on His righteousness. You choose to believe that His perfect justice will take care of you, just as you did when you were first born again.

Then, you can abide in Him by faith. Don't rely on your own crafty words or your own ideas. Even in our best-crafted strategies, we have limited knowledge. Have you noticed that? None of us has absolute knowledge. We don't know everything. But God does. When you let God defend you, you're no longer relying on your own works.

Fruit comes from abiding. It begins with an attitude of belief—a mindset. Then you must follow it with an attitude of dependence and humility. As you do, remember three principles.

First, believing is not so much a work as it is rest. Belief is actively resting on the promises of God. Resting in Him. Receiving, not doing. Abiding is patiently trusting Him.

Second, abiding involves an awareness of God's presence in our lives. Abiding is not a feeling. It's an acknowledgment that God is with you.

Finally, abiding involves surrender. When you abide in Jesus, you surrender your will to God's will. The alternative is placing yourself in the position of God. When you're not abiding in Him, you're doing things your own way. You're not trusting Him.

The habit of a moment-by-moment surrender to God is very fruitful. The fruit that God is looking for in our lives is not something we can produce ourselves.

ABIDING IS THE SOLUTION

The fruit of letting go of your past is not something you can produce on your own. You can't do it in your own strength. You can't get free from the past by running as fast as you can away from it. The solution is to abide in Christ.

Many of us get frustrated and upset because we remain so active. We work hard. We measure today's success by comparing it with yesterday. If we accomplished more, we feel good about ourselves. If we accomplished less, we feel bad. We offer our works to God to be well-pleasing to Him. For a time, it may look like it is working. We are able to keep up. But the reality is that failure is just up ahead.

Then what do you do when you fail? You stumble. You were depending on your own works. When you're not abiding, you depend on yourself. And you compare yourself with others to see how you're doing.

For example, if you go to a midweek service at your church, you will probably notice that there are fewer people in attendance than during a weekend service. You may be tempted to feel like you're better than those who didn't come. You may even think to yourself, *I made it to church. Where are all the slackers? What are they doing tonight?* And before you know it, you're in a position of judgment. You're judging yourself as better and others as worse. That state is not a place of abiding.

The place of abiding is evident when you have thoughts like, *It's so good to be in the house of the Lord. I want to be there as much as I can. And if I can't be there, wherever I am, I'll continue to abide in Jesus Christ. I'll abide in the presence of the Lord, and He in me*. You take to heart that "without Me," Jesus said, "you can do nothing" (John 15:5).

Jesus also said,

> If anyone does not abide in Me, he is cast out as a branch and is withered; and they gather them and throw them into the fire, and they are burned. If you abide in Me, and My words abide in you, you will ask what you desire, and it shall be done for you. By this My Father is glorified, that you bear much fruit; so you will be My disciples. As the Father loved Me, I also have loved you; abide in My love. If you keep My commandments, you will abide in My love, just as I have kept My Father's commandments and abide in His love (verses 6-10).

Did you know that the moment you were born again, you started abiding in Christ?

When I was born again, I didn't know the Bible. I didn't know how to pray either. I only knew that God loved me, He offered to forgive me of my sins through the finished work of Jesus Christ, and I needed to leave my sins. I had a very elementary view of God. I knew that God was God, and I was not. But I didn't know a lot. I didn't know where any of the books of the Bible were located. My family didn't even have a Bible in our house.

Yet, the finished work of Jesus Christ descended upon me at that moment in a very pure way. I didn't understand the word *abide* or know what the Greek word *meno* meant. But my pastor told me, "From now on, you're going to enjoy Jesus Christ for the rest of your life. He lives in you, and you live in Him."

And my response? "That's awesome! This is crazy. God is in me, and I am in Him?" I didn't walk away wondering, *What in the world does that mean?* Instead, I thought, *This is an amazing life. I wonder what else I need to learn. I wonder what's next?*

What happened? I had started with a simple, abiding relationship with Jesus Christ. My mindset began with thinking, *Jesus, You're so good to me. I'll do anything you say. Go anywhere you tell me. I'll live my life any way that you want. My life belongs to You.*

You see, if you abide in Jesus and His words abide in you, then you can ask for whatever you desire, and He'll give it to you (John 15:7). Jesus' words are life.

How many of us simply ask the Lord, "Please free me from my past." The key is to be abiding in Christ and to have His words abiding in you. How often? Moment by moment. It's an abiding *life*, not an abiding *act*. You are not surrendering to a one-time thing. You need to abide moment by moment. It's an abiding life, not a life filled with performance. It takes a lifetime of abiding.

Fruit develops in our lives, not through work, but through a relationship. God desires to work through us. God promises that if you are communing with Jesus, He will give you the desires of your heart. Your prayers will be answered.

To be clear, that doesn't mean you can name something from God and claim it. You can't decide you're going to claim your riches or claim your healing. Verse 7 has been twisted by some because they don't understand what Jesus is teaching here.

Jesus' teaching is very simple. As you abide in Christ moment by moment, His desires become your desires. Your prayers start to be in tune with Him. You begin asking for things that will glorify the Father. Your life reflects more and more of Jesus because you desire to do what pleases the Father.

It's the fruit of abiding, when you see your prayers answered. When I prayed with that person about his rent, I wasn't sure what God was going to do. But the desire of my heart at that moment was to pray that he would be able to pay his rent—to take his problem to the Lord. God was the One who could solve it.

Religious legalism is in the church today. It involves an air of criticism, nitpicking every point, and dividing the church. I don't know if you've noticed, but we live in a culture where people don't know how to disagree with one another without trying to destroy the other person. It's okay to have disagreements, even in the body of Christ.

Like-mindedness in the body of Christ doesn't mean that we agree on everything. That's called conformity. And the Bible says that we're only to be conformed to the image of Christ, not to one another. We don't want to become exact copies of each other. We want to become like Jesus. Being like-minded means that we generally agree with one another. And when we're like-minded, we can learn how to disagree in love.

The Bible doesn't say that the world will know we are disciples of Jesus because of our criticisms and our hyperjudgmental stances. No, Jesus said, "By this all will know that you are My disciples, if you have love for one another" (John 13:35). In fact, the Bible warns us not to bite and devour one another (Galatians 5:15). Can you imagine what that looks like? We must abide in Him.

Listen to a description of the Pharisees from Jesus' day:

> One distinctive feature of the Pharisees was their strong commitment to observing the law of God as it was interpreted and applied by the scribes. Although the priests had been responsible for teaching and interpreting the Law (Lev. 10:8-11; Deut. 33:8-10) in Old Testament times, many people had lost all respect for the priests because of the corruption in the Jerusalem priesthood. They looked to the scribes instead to interpret the Law for them. Some scribes were priests; many were not. Still, they lived pious, disciplined lives; and they had been trained to become experts in the Law. It was natural, then, for people to follow their leading rather than that of the priests.[2]

The Pharisees were dedicated men of the Word. But their problem was that they missed the intent of the Bible. Instead of hitting their hearts, it went right to their heads. They were theologically right; but in love and practice, they were very wrong. And Jesus condemned them for it. Jesus didn't tell those who were caught up in sin, "Woe to you." He told the Pharisees, "Woe to you" (see Matthew 23:13).

Let's look at an example of how God's Word missed the Pharisees' hearts. The Pharisees were very precise in their tithing. If they had a little garden with little mint bushes, they would make sure they tithed based on any growth (Matthew 23:23). But when their parents needed help, they would take money from their parents for financial gain (Matthew 15:3-9). They tithed their mint, but neglected their parents. The Pharisees were completely backward.

How did they miss it? They knew the Word, but the Word didn't abide in them. They were separated from Jesus Christ. If they had handled the Word properly, it would have brought them to Jesus. That's the whole purpose of the law—to point out your needs so it will point you to the Messiah. So the Pharisees could quote the Word to you. But the Word wasn't abiding in them. It wasn't in their hearts.

David wrote, "Your word I have hidden in my heart, that I might not sin against You" (Psalm 119:11). That's one of the advantages of memorizing Scripture. When you put God's Word in your heart, the Spirit of God can bring it back at the appropriate time and prevent you from sinning. Paul prayed that God "would grant you, according to the riches of His glory, to be strengthened with might through His Spirit in the inner man that Christ may dwell in your hearts through faith," and you would be rooted and grounded in love (Ephesians 3:16-17).

Eighteen inches can make all the difference. That 18 inches from your head to your heart—in your prayer life, in your evangelism, in your marriage, in your parenting, in your singleness, and in your abiding life—is life-changing. And it's only 18 inches. It's the difference between knowing something and experiencing it, between argumentation and heartbreak, and between contention and compassion. When you tend to argue, your heart's never touched by the needs around you. And, as a result, the needs around you are never touched by your heart.

The church of Jesus Christ is on the earth to represent God. And God's heart is always broken by sin. A compassionate heart always desires to help.

What's the difference between the heart and the head? Well, the heart doesn't let go of things so easily. It's at the core of who you are. Both the Hebrews and the Greeks believed this. It's the sum of your love and adoration. The heart speaks of the totality of your person.

Along with love and adoration, bitterness and contempt can reside in your heart. And it sticks there. That is why the Bible warns us against letting a root of bitterness spring up in our lives (Hebrews 12:15).

But what about our minds? Our minds are not so permanent. While our hearts tend to hold on to things, our mind changes. We probably change our minds a thousand times a day. On a dime, we change lanes. Or we change our drink order at a coffee shop. Our minds are constantly changing.

If the Word of God isn't abiding in our hearts, we will quickly change our minds away from the truth. When we move away from the truth, we're no longer abiding in Christ. And, if you pay attention, you almost always change your mind to benefit yourself, not to glorify the Father.

Letting go of your past is possible with an abiding life. Jesus said, "If anyone desires to come after Me, let him deny himself, and take up his cross, and follow Me" (Matthew 16:24). A life of abiding—of faith and dependence—brings great love and peace into your life. It results in a peace that surpasses all understanding.

Scripture says,

> Be anxious for nothing, but in everything by prayer and supplication, with thanksgiving, let your requests be made

> known to God; and the peace of God, which surpasses all understanding, will guard your hearts and minds through Christ Jesus (Philippians 4:6-7).

The abiding life is where peace is found. Be still and receive God's Word as unto the Lord.

Freedom from your past is found moment by moment as you abide in Christ. You know as well as I do that you can't undo the past any more than you can unscramble an egg. But you can live the life that God has given you at this moment. You can abide, trusting in Him. You can stay put, casting all your cares upon Him. You can search the Bible for passages that speak life to you—ones that relate to the sin issue in your life or to an issue that troubles you.

As another resource, you can find a list of scriptures that address different issues in your life like worry, anxiety, or fear at EdTaylor.org. The Bible has a lot to say about the things we deal with in our lives.

As you meditate on God's Word, confess it. Remain in Jesus. Trust Him. Enjoy your relationship with Him. Remember that God will do the work in your life as you abide in Him.

REFLECTION/DISCUSSION QUESTIONS

1. What does it mean to abide in Christ?
2. What does making your home *in Jesus* mean to you?
3. Think about a time that you chose to defend yourself. How did that go? Now, think about a time when you allowed God to be your defender. How did God work on your behalf?
4. What are some tactics that the enemy uses to get you to stop abiding in Jesus? What have you discovered or learned that will help you to fight against those tactics?

8

DEALING WITH SPIRITUAL WARFARE AND THE DEVIL

We all share many common issues in life. For example, we have bills to pay, family drama, and difficulties at work. We make mistakes and must contend with others' mistakes. However, as followers of Christ, we also face problems that others don't. It's true. For the believer, there is an added dimension of difficulty commonly referred to as spiritual warfare.

As my own pastor has told me, "To be forewarned is to be forearmed." In chapters 8 and 9, we will discuss spiritual warfare. In this chapter, I want to warn you about the spiritual battle you are engaged in. Then, in chapter 9, I want to show you how God has armed you to fight that battle.

There is a continual battle over our spiritual progress, our strength, and sometimes, even our sanity. It is vital to remember that we live on a battlefield and not on a playground. And on this battlefield, we face a three-faceted enemy: the world, the flesh, and the devil.

The *world* simply refers to the culture we live in—a culture that's antichrist. The word *antichrist* doesn't only refer to the individual Antichrist who is to come. Instead, the prefix *anti* has two meanings.

The first is "against." Our culture is against Christ. Jesus described the pressure and push from culture as hating Him (John 15:18). This world's thoughts and actions are antichrist. They are against the things of God.

The second meaning for *anti* is "in place of." This world has many substitutes for God, such as the belief that the universe was created randomly, without a Creator. These substitutes take away your devotion and dedication to God.

At any stage of life, you can get caught up in the world. As you breathe the air of culture's influence in and out, you pick up ideas from your family, your friends, and even, the church. And you may not realize that some of the beliefs you've collected are, in fact, antichrist. Meaning they don't agree or align with what God says about Himself. To protect ourselves, we must dedicate ourselves to reading the Bible and living with our eyes wide open. Carefully evaluate the ideas that surround you through a biblically faithful lens and a biblical worldview.

Not only is the world against us, but our flesh is as well. Remember in chapter 3, we discussed this in detail. When I am talking about the flesh here, I'm not talking about your physical body. When the Bible uses the word *flesh* spiritually, it speaks of your old, sinful habit patterns.

You see the flesh when you're wronged or in a difficult situation. It's your initial, automatic response in those circumstances. Your old, sinful habits don't reflect the love of Jesus or His presence in your life. Back to our driving example from chapter 6, after being cut off, if you start cussing the other driver out, that's your flesh. That's not from God. Nor is waving to them with one finger.

If you live in the flesh, you tend to be angry and frustrated. You likely respond to people and circumstances in ways that make you ineffective for God's kingdom. When you're walking in the flesh, you're not pleasing God. You must learn to walk in the Spirit and not to fulfill the lust of the flesh (Galatians 5:16).

The third enemy against us is the devil. Satan uses the world to provoke our flesh in an attempt to get us to compromise, positioning us against the things of God. That compromise weakens the church, marriages, and families.

The devil has many different names in the Bible.

- In Ephesians 4:27, he's referred to as "the devil."
- In 1 John 5:19 (NLT), he's known as the "evil one."
- In 2 Corinthians 4:4, he's called "the god of this age."
- In John 8:44 (NLT), Jesus referred to him as "the father of lies," which means he's the origin of all lies. Lies are birthed from the devil himself.
- In Revelation 12:10, he's known as "the accuser of our brethren."
- In Matthew 4:3, he's referred to as "the tempter."
- In Luke 22:3, he's called "Satan."

The devil is a real, created being.

THE DEVIL—IN DETAIL

The Gospel of Luke records an interaction that reveals an important insight into how the devil goes about his work. Jesus told Simon Peter, "Simon, Simon! Indeed, Satan has asked for you, that he may sift you as wheat. But I have prayed for you, that your faith should not fail; and when you have returned to Me, strengthen your brethren" (Luke 22:31-32). Jesus warned Peter that the devil had asked specifically for him, and that he wanted to separate Peter from Jesus.

The listeners of the day would have understood the illustration Jesus used. At the time, it was a common experience to sift wheat.

They would take the top and beat it to separate the kernels from the husk, the wheat from the chaff. It is a refining process that is necessary to enjoy the wheat. In other words, Jesus told Peter, "Hey, Satan's asked for you. He wants to beat you down. And he wants to separate you from Me."

But notice that Jesus gave Peter a little insight into how the process would play out. Satan was going to have some success. Jesus included, "When you have returned to Me..."

Unfortunately, the devil does experience some success among us. The sifting of wheat for Peter started with his denial of his Savior—not once, but three times. That denial resulted in all sorts of emotions and mind games. It left Peter vulnerable to the wicked schemes of the devil. Satan's attempt to separate Peter's faithfulness from Jesus was temporarily successful.

Like Peter, you are also in a very real battle. In Ephesians 6:12, the Bible says, "We do not wrestle against flesh and blood, but against principalities, against powers, against the rulers of the darkness of this age, against spiritual hosts of wickedness in the heavenly places." You and I are wrestling against forces and powers of darkness. You need to put on the whole armor of God to make it through.

Too often, we think the battle is with another person. For example, some husbands and wives treat each other like enemies. They are not enemies. Instead, there's a spiritual reality working behind their relationship that is desperately trying to separate them.

As soon as you open your eyes to the real battle, victory begins. But until then, you'll find yourself taking matters into your own hands. For example, you may try to get back at someone for something they did or try to prove your point in an argument. When you do that, you'll never experience the victory that's already yours by faith. Think about how healthy our churches would be if we remembered that the root issue is not among the people. It's the enemy trying to separate us by using our personalities and sinful mistakes against us.

The Bible describes the Antichrist who is to come. It says that he's one "who opposes and exalts himself above all that is called God or that is worshiped, so that he sits as God in the temple of God, showing himself that he is God" (2 Thessalonians 2:4). The Antichrist that is being described here is indwelt by the devil himself. He personifies the devil's attribute of opposing God and anything about God, including God's followers.

The devil is not your friend. Neither is the world's culture or your flesh. The devil likes to oppose God's work in your life. He'll try to discourage and distract you so that you go offtrack, no longer usable in God's hands.

It's important to note that the devil is not all-powerful. He is not the opposite of God. He is a created being. Satan's power is limited by God. God's power is unlimited. Yet, the devil does have more power than an unregenerate or unsaved man or woman. An unbeliever is no match for the devil. As a result, an unsaved person can be possessed by the devil.

Not only is the devil limited in his power, but also, he cannot be everywhere at once. It is additionally important to note that the devil is singular. For that reason, most of us have never faced the devil head-on. Likely, the devil must prioritize his presence in the battles that he wages in the spiritual realm.

However, Satan does have some help. When the devil rebelled against God, he took a third of the angels of heaven with him. Those fallen, rebellious angels are demons. They live in the demonic realm. The principalities and powers referred to in Ephesians 6:12 are demons. And certainly, the believer has experience in fighting demonic opposition all throughout their lives.

While Satan's power is limited, let me warn you. Just as an unregenerate person is no match for the devil, neither are you when you are operating in your own strength and wisdom. The devil will wipe you out.

There are two errors humans make concerning the demonic realm.

One is getting themselves hyped up and exaggerating it. That's a mistake. On the other end of the spectrum is minimizing the demonic realm and spiritual warfare. That is also a mistake.

Although you're no match for the devil in your own strength, he is no match for the power of God in you. As a child of God, you do not need to fear the devil. You don't need to back down from him or run away and cower in fear. You have victory through Jesus Christ. And you can trust God to protect you.

When life gets hard, believers can be vulnerable to false teachers who promise deliverance from the things they are going through. One false teaching claims that believers can be demon-possessed. That's not true in any way. As a believer in Jesus Christ, you are sealed, guarded, protected, and indwelled by God Himself—100 percent! Light and darkness cannot coexist.

As it says in 1 John 4:4, "You are of God, little children, and have overcome them, because He who is in you is greater than he who is in the world." This verse not only declares God's power, but it reveals who is in you (God) and where the devil is (in the world). And the one who is in the world does not reside in the believer, not even 1 percent.

So you don't need a "deliverance ministry." The enemy can oppress and harass believers, but he can never possess them. Believers belong to Jesus Christ. If you're a believer, Jesus purchased you with His blood. And He indwells you now with His Holy Spirit.

Remember, Jesus described the devil as a thief who only comes "to steal, and to kill, and to destroy" (John 10:10). He will take anything and everything you give him. He'll occupy any space that you leave open for him.

THE DEVIL'S DEVICES

To help us be prepared, we need to know how he'll attack us in spiritual battles. We need to be prepared "lest Satan should take advantage of us; for we are not ignorant of his devices" (2 Corinthians 2:11). With that in mind, here are eight devices the devil will use against you.

1. The devil attacks you relentlessly.

Activity in the demonic realm never stops. When Peter returned to Jesus after being sifted, he wrote, "Be sober, be vigilant; because your adversary the devil walks about like a roaring lion, seeking whom he may devour" (1 Peter 5:8). That's a vivid picture. The devil is always hungry and always looking for someone to destroy.

What does that look like in our lives? Let's say you experience a victory against Satan in the morning. After you wake up, you have a thought inspired by the flesh and you pray against it. You walk in victory going down the stairs. But before you open your cereal box, the thought is back. And it's constant. Then, your kids act out, and now you're mad. Then, the phone rings. Then, you are interrupted by your neighbor. Then, your boss—frustration after frustration. And at that point you're thinking, *Oh, man...*

If you have victory in the morning, the devil returns at noon. When you are victorious at noon, he's back at one o'clock, reminding you of what happened both that morning and of what happened at noon. It simply doesn't stop.

Think about it this way: First, the devil knocks on your front door. You slam the door in his face and you think, *I'm done with him.* But then, he walks around your house and tries to enter through the back door. You run to the back of the house and you slam the door there too—and lock it. But later, you find he's trying to climb through a window. That's the relentless attack of the enemy.

The devil doesn't cease his attacks against a child of God. He's always looking for an opening, for even the smallest hint of compromise or faithlessness. He's looking for something he can capitalize on. And why does it get so hard to deal with? Because we frequently don't pay attention to the little things. We brush them off as if they're no big deal. A small compromise here. A little wayward look there. An intrusive thought. Or a flippant word. No big deal, right?

For example, once again, remember that illustration of being cut off in traffic (chapter 6). Even a very small thing can cause us to allow our anger to change us into a different person. Given the enemy's character, do you think he's not going to use that against you? Of course he will. Certainly, he would capitalize on even the smallest of openings to try to defeat you.

Another time the enemy will approach you is when you decide that you want to get right with the Lord. You decide, "I never want to do that again. I want to walk in the Spirit." And then, the enemy will accuse you. He'll say something like, "You vile, wicked person. Look at your heart. Look at your mind. What did you just do? What did you do last week? You'll never be good enough." Satan hates when we are focused on being faithful.

Attacks from the enemy are constant. They're relentless. We must remember that the territory we take from the enemy in the name of Jesus Christ must be held fast in the name of Jesus Christ. You can't let your guard down, not even for a second. You can't rely on past victories. You need victory now—in every moment. If you don't hold territory gained, the devil will take it back. And he'll bring his friends with him. Jesus spoke about this (Matthew 12:43-45). Then, the attacks will be worse than they were before. Satan only yields what he must and seeks to retake it all.

2. The devil attacks you physically.

We observe how the devil physically attacks us through the life of Job. When God removed His guard from around Job, Satan began to attack him physically. We read in Job 2:7-8, "Satan went out from the presence of the LORD, and struck Job with painful boils from the sole of his foot to the crown of his head. And he took for himself a potsherd with which to scrape himself while he sat in the midst of the ashes."

The devil can attack us physically if God allows it. Don't misunderstand me, the devil is not behind every physical issue. Sin is behind every physical issue. However, our physical circumstances are a tool Satan can use. And if he's not bringing a physical challenge upon us, he can use our physical weaknesses against us.

Consider this, let's say you're generally in good health. But then, you get sick. The sickness is serious enough to place you in the hospital. Doctors run tests and give you a diagnosis. Even though the doctors say you will be okay, the diagnosis still messes with your head. You're not sure. You're worried and confused. The devil can use physical circumstances to challenge you.

But, like in the case of Job, the devil can also bring them. Jesus attributed many, but not all, physical infirmities to demonic activity. For example, the woman who was bent over for 18 years (Luke 13:11). Jesus said, "Ought not this woman, being a daughter of Abraham, whom Satan has bound—think of it—for eighteen years, be loosed from this bond on the Sabbath?" (Luke 13:16). The enemy bound her. Satan can attack us physically.

3. The devil attacks you financially.

Money is a big issue in spiritual warfare. It's a bigger issue than the church will often admit. Money is a big deal.

The devil can attack you financially in one of two ways. First, he can attack you through a lack of money. Again, we learn that from Job. Everything he had was taken away. In a moment, Job lost all his cattle, sheep, and oxen. He was stripped of everything and ripped off by the devil.

> Job arose, tore his robe, and shaved his head; and he fell to the ground and worshiped. And he said: "Naked I came from my mother's womb, and naked shall I return there. The Lord gave, and the Lord has taken away; blessed

> be the name of the Lord." In all this Job did not sin or charge God with wrong (Job 1:20-22).

At the end of the trial, Job passed the test. God restored Job tenfold. But the devil was behind his loss.

Another way the devil can use a lack of money against you is challenging your faith in God's provision. When you lack money, you start to worry. You don't know what you're going to do, and you start to freak out. You get anxious. You question whether God will provide.

Second, the devil can use money to attack you when you have more than you need. You start to trust in your money instead of in God. You stop looking to God and pressing into Him. Be careful. Are you making financial decisions instead of spiritual ones? If you are, your eyes aren't on the Lord. Money can take our eyes away from our faith.

Money is a large part of our lives. We need it to live. But if you don't learn to honor God with your money, you won't honor Him at all. You can't live a dual life.

4. The devil attacks your mind.

The mind is a battleground for your life. There are only two options when fighting here. Will you believe God's truth? Or will you believe the lies thrown at you by the world, your flesh, and the devil?

Isaiah 26:3 says, "You will keep him in perfect peace, whose mind is stayed on You, because he trusts in You." That's a promise from God. When your mind is stayed on Him, you'll live in perfect peace.

In contrast, the devil loves to disrupt this peace by attacking your mind. He'll try to influence what you think about God. You may have thoughts that come out of nowhere. Thoughts such as, *It's not fair, Lord.* Or, *God doesn't even care. He's abandoned me.*

The devil loves to inspire doubts about God's faithfulness. He introduces anxious thoughts, worries that God won't care for you or your family. He'll inspire beliefs that overwhelm you and distance you from a place of faith. It can feel like an onslaught.

Yet, the devil doesn't perform this work from the inside. He is not resident in your mind, messing with your brain. He does his work from the outside. Often, he merely needs to kickstart the process, and you will take it from there. He sows seeds of doubt about your situation. Circumstances where any logical person would look at the situation and say, "This is horrible. We'll never survive. We'll never get out of this."

But that's viewing your situation through the eyes of the world. When I take off my glasses, I can't see clearly. But when I put my glasses on, the objects around me come into focus. It is the same with the glasses of faith. When you put them on, truth becomes clear. You'll see that you can trust God with your situation. God can make a way where there is no way. He has resources at His disposal that you don't. You need Him. In those challenges, you must look through the lenses of faith to believe God's truth.

Remember God's promise. He'll keep you in perfect peace when your mind is focused on Him. When you're dedicated to seeking the Lord, He will honor His word. As you're thinking about Him, He gives you peace. He's going to take care of tough circumstances. You can trust Him. He has brought you this far, and He's not going to dump you now.

A lack of peace stems from a choice to doubt His promise. When you believe the lie, you think things like, *This is the end of me.* Or, *This will never end.* Then, you start exaggerating the problem. If the devil can get you to believe a lie, you'll live in that lie—in rebellion against and compromise from your loving God. We must protect our minds constantly.

That's why it's so important for us to know God's truth. But to know that truth, you must read your Bible. Scripture is where God reveals His truth to us. The Bible is more important than a good sermon or moving worship music. It's the most important book in your life.

The Bible teaches you about God's character and nature. It shows you how He's come through for people in situations harder than yours. God's faithfulness encourages us in the midst of what we're going through. Widely, the church is weak today because believers aren't in the Word of God.

5. The devil attacks your emotions.

This device of the devil goes hand in hand with how Satan attacks your mind. And it's a heavy-duty tactic for the enemy as it is deployed when we are at our most vulnerable. Our emotions are powerful. They move us. So the enemy loves to stir up feelings of distrust, fear, and anxiety. Those emotions undermine your faith in God. If you're not regularly in God's Word, then the faith that's there will be wiped away by your feelings.

When you talk with others, listen to yourself. If you're always talking about how you feel, you've been living through your feelings. That's not inherently good or bad, but be careful; the enemy loves to exploit your feelings. Here's why: Our feelings are real. You can't talk someone out of what they're feeling—whether it's strong or weak, sad or happy. The trouble is that our feelings don't always tell us the truth about a situation.

I'll give you a great example: cartoon movies. When you watch one of these movies, you can feel a range of emotions, such as a cartoon character can make you cry. The character is fake; the story is not real. But the film has been carefully crafted by professionals who know how to put movies together well. And you can get caught up in the story. It's a cartoon. Yet, it can evoke real emotions inside you that don't tell you the truth. The truth is that you are watching a made-up cartoon. It's not real. So truly, there is nothing to be sad about.

The devil loves to exploit your emotions. And if you get caught up in them, you may not be able to tell why you're feeling a certain way. When you are in God's Word, you will be tethered to His steadfastness. As it says in Romans 10:17, "Faith comes by hearing, and hearing by the word of God." His Word works in you as you read it (1 Thessalonians 2:13).

Also, your emotions can make you focus solely on the problem in front of you. Have you noticed this in your life? The more you look at a problem, the bigger it gets. It blinds you to the truth of who God is.

Then, anxiety and worry create problems that never materialize. We can take a small thing and make it so big, even when the little thing didn't occur in the first place. The enemy exploits our real-life, human issues when we separate ourselves (when we're sifted away) from God—away from the tether of abiding in Christ.

Emotions come in all shapes and sizes. And negative ones come from the pit of hell. Discouragement. Hopelessness. Worry. Defeat. Depression. Sorrow. Even suicidal thoughts. It's all part of spiritual warfare. Suicidal thoughts don't come from God. They arise when you're hopeless. Your emotions stir up false thoughts like, *It would be better if I go. The world will be better without me.*

Those are lies from the one who Jesus called "the father of lies" (John 8:44 NLT). They're not true. Things wouldn't be better without you. Your family and friends would be hurt for the rest of their lives. It would bring another layer of spiritual warfare where they wonder, *What could I have done?*

Suicidal thoughts are not from the Lord. The truth is that the Lord is ready to save and rescue you. The only way to be safe and secure is to trust in the Lord.

6. The devil attacks you with confusion.

The devil uses confusion and uncertainty to keep you off balance and in retreat. When you don't know what to do, the devil loves to keep you in a perpetual state of indecision and inactivity.

On occasion, when I'm sitting down with someone in a discipleship conversation, they will say something like, "I'm so confused."

And I'll stop them right there. That statement reveals the root of the issue in our conversation because that confusion did not come from the Lord. "God is not the author of confusion but of peace" (1 Corinthians 14:33). When you're confused, it affects every part of your life. I will follow that statement by asking, "What are you confused about?"

Lately, I often hear things like, "I'm confused, pastor. I don't know where I'm supposed to live. I think God's calling me to move to another state. I just don't know."

So I'll ask them, "What's your address?" When they tell me, I'll reply, "Well then, go home. That's where you live today. That is not so confusing." At first, they are thrown off.

The person will reply, "No, you don't understand. I'm not sure if I'm supposed to go." Then I'll ask, "Do you think you should go?" They'll answer, "I think so. I'm so confused." So I'll tell them, "Then move, and tell me how it goes."

The decision that is in front of them is a step of faith. It is important and life changing. When you seek the Lord in it, He will grant you wisdom. However, in the midst of a decision like that you don't need to be confused. Until you leave for a different place, go home to the place where you live right now.

You can see how the enemy will take something you're not quite sure about and take the opportunity to introduce confusion into the mix. Now, sometimes confusion is simply a matter of not really understanding the situation. That is not what we are discussing here. No, the confusion that trips you up is one that blurs your mind, making you unwilling to obey what you know to be true. You're trying to discern the will of God. It could be God's will for you to move, or it might not. But why are you worried about tomorrow?

Remember when the devil tried to bring confusion to Peter in Matthew 16:21-23? Peter knew Jesus was the Messiah. He, at this time, had already left everything to follow Jesus. He had witnessed the miracles, heard Jesus' teachings, and devoted his entire life to following Jesus.

Yet, in his mind, which came out of his mouth, he rebuked Jesus, confused about the truth that Jesus had just said. It was clear. Jesus is going to Jerusalem and will suffer many things. The simple response from Jesus was to get behind Him. He brought clarity very quickly and by His rebuke showed the source of Peter's confusion was the devil himself. A word of clarity will help clear up confusion. That's why reading your Bible and praying every day is so important.

Jesus told us not to worry about tomorrow. As you deal with today, follow Jesus' command, "Do not worry about tomorrow, for tomorrow will worry about its own things. Sufficient for the day is its own trouble" (Matthew 6:34).

You know where you live. There's no need to be confused. If you want to discern God's will, that's a different thing. But you can see that through a decision that would be a beautiful, wonderful step of faith to stay or to go, you've allowed the enemy to confuse you.

If you can learn not to worry about tomorrow, you won't be confused today. Confusion is not from the Lord. It's from the enemy. In confusion, the devil starts to pressure you to make decisions that are not made by faith. And if you are not making decisions by faith, it won't please the Lord (Hebrews 11:6).

7. The devil attacks you spiritually.

You relate to God in the Spirit. You're spiritually connected to Him. Because of this connection, the devil is always trying to sever that tie.

Using lies, emotions, mind games, and confusion, the enemy of your soul will tell you that God doesn't love you anymore. Or he'll put into question what you know about God's character, like he did with Eve in the garden by asking, "Has God indeed said?" (Genesis 3:1). The devil will try to convince you that God's grace isn't real.

Again, we look at the psalmist in Psalm 73. He said, "Truly God is good to Israel, to such as are pure in heart. But as for me, my feet had almost stumbled; my steps had nearly slipped" (Psalm 73:1-2).

Even a psalmist dealt with it. It's like he was saying, "I know God is good, but I almost fell hard."

In his case, we know what happened. The psalmist was looking at people around him who were prospering, even though they hated God. It messed with his head. He knew that God was good. But as he started comparing his life to theirs, his feet almost stumbled. If you read the rest of the psalm, you'll see that he went into the sanctuary of the Lord and got his eyes focused back on God. Then, he understood what he saw and trusted the Lord.

8. The devil attacks you wildly.

The devil executes an all-out blitz against you. He doesn't attack in just one area. He will hit you in one area of your life. Then, he'll hit you in another. He's relentless (recall device 1).

An illustration that comes to mind is a military tactic utilized in air warfare—carpet bombing. A tactic especially relied upon during World War II, squadrons of large aircraft would be loaded with thousands of pounds of bombs. These bomber groups would be assigned a large area to drop their entire payloads over. Factories, city centers, infrastructure, churches, and homes were all destroyed with countless lives lost. The result of the onslaught completely devastated the places that were targeted. Satan dumps his attacks on you all at once to see if he can wipe you out. He has a scorched-earth policy. He'll take as much ground as you will give him.

It's easy to be overwhelmed by the enemy's attacks. When you're not feeling well physically, he starts throwing negative thoughts in your head. When you begin to react to situations solely by feelings, your faith is weakened. Then, you find yourself in a situation where you're mad at someone you love. On top of that, you're fearful because of bad news from the doctor. And sometimes you wonder, *When is this all going to end?*

That's a great question. As a pastor, I must tell you the truth. Never—not on this side of eternity. The deliverance that is yours in Christ comes when you shed your earthly body and enter His presence. Until then, there will be a battle—a fight for your spiritual growth.

But through it all, remember we are not helpless. We need to remind ourselves of God's faithfulness and power in our lives. The Bible says, in Isaiah 59:19, "So shall they fear the name of the LORD from the west, and His glory from the rising of the sun; when the enemy comes in like a flood, the Spirit of the LORD will lift up a standard against him."

The enemy is not going to be victorious. When you are under severe attack, God will come in and raise up a standard of protection. He will defend you in the battle. When you feel like you're trapped—like there's no way out—remember that God makes a way where there is no way. Learn to look to Him and trust Him. He will give you perfect peace as your mind is stayed on Him.

REFLECTION/DISCUSSION QUESTIONS

1. Knowing your real enemies are Satan and his demons, how will this change your approach to conflict?
2. Which one of the eight tactics that the enemy uses do you find yourself most vulnerable to? Why?
3. How does being aware of some of the devil's limitations equip you to stand strong against him?

9

DEALING WITH SPIRITUAL WARFARE—HOW TO WAGE THE BATTLE

As we learned in the previous chapter, we are in the middle of a spiritual battle. The devil doesn't want you to grow spiritually. He doesn't want you to be effective for God's kingdom.

The devil attacks us relentlessly, physically, and financially. He attacks our minds and our emotions. Satan loves to exploit confusion. He attacks us spiritually by trying to separate us from God. And he attacks us wildly, hitting us at every turn.

In his attacks, the devil plays dirty. He doesn't abide by the rules. It's as simple as that.

But lest we give the devil too much attention, we must remember God's faithfulness. Yes, there's a battle going on. But Christians always fight from a place of victory. Paul says, in Romans 8:37, "In all these things we are more than conquerors through Him who loved us."

You don't fight *to* victory. You fight *from* victory because Jesus Christ paid the price and rose from the dead. He is the eternal King of kings and Lord of lords. You can trust Him with your life. Because of what Jesus did, you can "fight the good fight of faith" (1 Timothy 6:12). You are not alone in the fight. And truly, it's not even our fight. Safeguarding victory is not our burden to shoulder. Jesus is our defender.

As you fight from a place of victory, here are eight ways to defeat the enemy's attacks in your life.

1. WE DEFEAT THE DEVIL BY FIGHTING THE RIGHT BATTLE

Often, we fight the wrong battles with the wrong weapons in the wrong places. The battle is spiritual, not personal. Because so many of the challenges in our lives include other people, much of the spiritual warfare in your life will be attached to a person.

You may have difficulties at work, problems in your neighborhood, family dramas, and church issues. Many of these circumstances pit a person against another person. And because of that, we falsely conclude that our battle is with that person.

However, the battle is not with that person. We are not each other's enemies. The devil attempts to divide us. He wants to get people mad at each other so that we are busy constantly bickering. That is not God's will. The Bible warns, "If you bite and devour one another, beware lest you be consumed by one another!" (Galatians 5:15).

The battle is spiritual. In Ephesians 6:12, we read, "We do not wrestle against flesh and blood, but against principalities, against powers, against the rulers of the darkness of this age, against spiritual hosts of wickedness in the heavenly places." So anytime you're striving against people, struggling with others, or wrestling against individuals, you are fighting the wrong battle. Don't get sidetracked from the real battle by fighting against others.

Too frequently, Christians waste so much time and energy in fighting each another—church members fighting one another, pastors competing against other pastors, congregations provoking other congregations, denominations warring against other denominations. It's all worthless. When you participate in these quarrels, you're making things worse, not better.

The enemy uses spiritual forces to aggravate situations and escalate them out of proportion. We're fighting against a well-organized horde of demons. The battle is won by abiding in Christ—by loving God first and then loving our neighbor.

2. WE DEFEAT THE DEVIL BY RESISTING HIM

You need to actively and regularly resist the devil. As James said, "Submit to God. Resist the devil and he will flee from you" (James 4:7). That's both an instruction and a promise.

In the midst of spiritual warfare, there is no time to be passive—to throw up your hands in defeat and discouragement. Don't tell yourself things like, *This is the way it's always going to be. I'm always going to be defeated, discouraged, and depressed.*

No, instead, resist the devil and he will flee from you. The word *resist* means to stand against, to stand firm. It means to stand strong. Don't retreat or give up any territory. I know the fight gets overwhelming and hard. But when that occurs, it is not the time to collapse. Resist the enemy. Push back. Say no to temptations.

The greatest word in your vocabulary that you can use to resist the devil is *no*. So much temptation and sin can be avoided when we learn to say no. "No, I won't say that." "No, I won't listen to that." "No, I won't go there." "No, I won't do that." "No."

The Bible describes the devil as "walk[ing] about like a roaring lion, seeking whom he may devour" (1 Peter 5:8). Stand fast and stare him down. Resist him. The next time the devil tries to remind you of your past, you remind him of his future. He knows what's coming.

When Satan comes in, you call his bluff. He has been a liar and a thief from the beginning. Have faith, confidence, contentment, peace, and trust in God. Resist the devil, and he will run away.

You don't need to run away; that's the territory God has given to you. The devil is the enemy. God promises that Satan will be the one running away. You don't have to run. Stand your ground.

3. WE DEFEAT THE DEVIL WITH OBEDIENCE

We give the enemy a lot of ground through disobedience and compromise. We make things harder for ourselves when we choose to disobey God. When we dabble in spiritual things and we're *religious*, we aren't in *relationship* with Jesus. We give up territory for no good reason.

The battle is hard enough without giving up terrain to the enemy. If you take a step toward disobedience, likely where will your next step be? Disobedience. The longer you continue, the farther you go in the wrong direction.

The Bible tells us, "Though we walk in the flesh, we do not war according to the flesh. For the weapons of our warfare are not carnal" (2 Corinthians 10:3-4). The weapons we need to fight the spiritual battle aren't human. Instead, those weapons are

> mighty in God for pulling down strongholds, casting down arguments and every high thing that exalts itself against the knowledge of God, bringing every thought into captivity to the obedience of Christ, and being ready to punish all disobedience when your obedience is fulfilled (verses 4-6).

It is important to take every thought captive. Assess your thoughts. If any of them aren't true, replace the lie with the truth. Then choose to walk in obedience to Christ. If you did this, you will experience victory right away.

But when the enemy shoots a thought laced with a falsehood your way, and you don't take it captive, you begin to dwell on it. Then, that thought becomes an emotion, and you feel it. And before you know it, you get overcome with your wrong thoughts and feelings. As a result, you've distanced yourself away from the Lord.

God arms us to fight the spiritual battle. We are not weak and helpless. The Bible is a powerful weapon that He gives us. We must use Scripture by

- reading it every day
- memorizing it—hiding it in your heart so you won't sin against God (Psalm 119:11)
- applying it—living out what you read in your actions
- learning how to study it

In short, learn God's truth, and then, replace the lies of the devil with the truth.

I must warn you. Taking your thoughts captive can be tiring. It means constantly being deliberate and intentional with all your thoughts. It's hard work. That's why many people choose not to do it. Yet, it's better to be tired obeying God than to be disobedient with any amount of energy. The Bible reminds us, "Let us not grow weary while doing good, for in due season we shall reap if we do not lose heart" (Galatians 6:9).

4. WE DEFEAT THE DEVIL WITH OUR FAITH

Our steadfast trust in God causes the devil to back down. Trusting God is a mighty weapon in the spiritual battle. Why else would the devil want you to believe his lies? When you believe them, you're powerless.

Not only are you powerless when you believe a lie, your faith wanes. We are weak when we walk around as believers who don't believe God. Instead, we need to walk by faith.

The Holy Spirit is the author of the Bible. Listen to what the Holy Spirit inspired Peter to write: "Resist [the devil], steadfast in the faith, knowing that the same sufferings are experienced by your brotherhood in the world" (1 Peter 5:9).

The phrase "steadfast in the faith" can refer to your personal faith. You're a born-again believer. You are a new creation in Christ. Old things have passed away, behold, all things have become new (2 Corinthians 5:17).

But it can also mean a steadfastness in believing God and His Word. You are equipped by not only knowing that your faith has connected you with God and your sins are forgiven, but also, a steadfastness in believing Him at His Word. When God said through James, "Resist the devil and he will flee from you" (James 4:7), believe it! Trust what God has said.

You don't need to remain caught up by the things the world says you'll never be healed from or that the world says you'll never get over. God can do a work that man cannot. God will change us on the inside; He transforms us. And if God doesn't do it instantly, the Bible promises that we are in the process of being sanctified. All of us are being changed over time. We are living testimonies.

We defeat the devil with our faith. "Whatever is born of God overcomes the world. And this is the victory that has overcome the world—our faith" (1 John 5:4). That's where victory comes from. It comes from choosing to believe what God says and acting on that faith.

In Hebrews, we read about men and women who were exactly like you and me. What do we learn from them? They acted by faith—time and time again.

Hebrews 11 begins, "Faith is the substance of things hoped for, the evidence of things not seen. For by it the elders obtained a good testimony" (Hebrews 11:1-2). Do you desire a good testimony? It comes by faith—by trusting God, believing Him, resisting the devil, and refusing to believe the devil's lies.

5. WE DEFEAT THE DEVIL WITH THE NAME OF JESUS CHRIST

Our victory comes through the name of Jesus. Scripture tells us about a time when Michael the archangel was fighting the devil about the body of Moses (Jude 9). Now, I don't know *why* that was taking place. The Bible doesn't say. But what a skirmish it must have been.

When this event occurred, even Michael didn't face the devil head-on fighting fire with fire. Jude 9 says, "Michael the archangel, in contending with the devil...dared not bring against him a reviling accusation, but said, 'The Lord rebuke you!'"

Michael knew that it was the power of God that would defeat the devil. This is important to remember. On television, people are creating fanciful, weird, and false doctrines about how to deal with the devil. They're yelling at the devil, kicking the devil, screaming at the devil, and more. A few years ago, there was even a person who claimed that he had the devil in his hand—whirling him around his head and throwing him out.

This must stop. You simply resist the devil. God will take care of him.

For example, let's say you wake up in the middle of the night because you had a nightmare. The room is dark. You're anxious and you hear noises. You don't know what's going on or what to do. In that moment, declare the name of Jesus Christ. Pray to Him. A prayer like, *I love You, Jesus. You are in this room with me. You dwell with me. The blood of Jesus Christ covers this home, covers this room, and covers my kids. And I hold fast to You.*

The name of Jesus will rebuke the devil anywhere—in your bedroom, in your car, and even in your cubicle. The Bible says, "Nor is there salvation in any other, for there is no other name under heaven given among men by which we must be saved" (Acts 4:12).

We must remember what occurred when Jesus sent out 70 of His disciples. He gave them the authority to heal, preach, help, and serve. They returned with joy, saying, "Lord, even the demons are subject to us in Your name" (Luke 10:17).

The name of Jesus is powerful. The name of Jesus is strong. Recall, "The name of the LORD is a strong tower; the righteous run to it and are safe" (Proverbs 18:10). There is safety in the name of Jesus Christ.

Could it be that you are under the weight of attack and difficulty, yet time after time, you've forgotten that there's power in the name of Jesus Christ? When you look at your problems, do they seem so big that you don't even see God anymore?

When you are under attack, instead of focusing on your problems, stand back and say, "You know what? The Lord rebuke you. You don't own this house. You don't own my family. You don't own this world. Do you think you are the god of this age? You're not. Because King Jesus is coming back, and I have hope in Him."

There's power in the name of Jesus. Let His name and your God-given identity be the strength that holds you firm and helps you stand when the enemy comes in like a flood.

We live in a culture where the big issue of the day is identity. Why? I believe the devil knows this truth: When you know who you are in Christ, you live according to your God-given identity and, therefore, fulfill God's destiny for your life. Satan doesn't want that.

We often refer to the will of God. But I like the word *destiny*. I think it better describes what God wants to do in your life. What has God done in your life as a believer? You're a new creation. You are clean. You are washed. You are strong. You are protected. The list goes on.

But if you're not careful, you'll miss the opportunity. Now, the enemy is lying to boys, girls, and their parents by telling them that they can create their *own* identity. Although that lie may be possible to vainly pursue, it's not the will of God. He has given you your identity. Like Jeremiah, God knew you before He formed you in the womb, and He has a plan for your life (Jeremiah 1:5).

I know part of the spiritual warfare waged by Satan comes at us from our culture. It's heavy. It's hard. It's difficult. Remember, our threefold enemy is the world, the flesh, and the devil. But you were born for this moment, friend. You are an ambassador that the Lord appointed for this very time.

We need to seize the day and walk forward in love. We need to connect this confused, upside-down culture with the love of Jesus Christ—one person at a time. Not only has God sent His only begotten Son to die on your behalf and forgive you—by faith—of all your sins, but He has given you an identity to walk in each day.

If you come to Him, you can leave your hopelessness behind. You can leave your anger and frustrations behind. You can move past the addictions and the challenges. You can set them down and follow Jesus Christ. Don't stray from the purpose He has drawn you to. Jesus will help you live in such a way to fulfill His destiny for your life.

6. WE DEFEAT THE DEVIL WITH THE WORD OF GOD

We cannot underestimate the value of this tool for fighting the enemy. Scripture is the truth. God's Word is powerful. Hebrews 4:12 says, "The word of God is living and powerful, and sharper than any two-edged sword, piercing even to the division of soul and spirit, and of joints and marrow, and is a discerner of the thoughts and intents of the heart."

Truth is a mighty weapon. Our culture says, "You have your truth. I have mine. We all have our own truth." But that's false. There is only *one* truth. Jesus declared, "I am the way, the truth, and the life. No one comes to the Father except through Me" (John 14:6).

Of course, there are many opinions about the truth. But if you choose to live the lie that you can make up your own truth, you're denying *the* truth and setting aside a powerful weapon in the spiritual battle. *The* truth vanquishes all lies. Immediately. And we get that truth from God's Word.

Now, we must remain alert to nuanced deception surrounding this. I want you to be careful. Some will say that the Bible contains the truth of God. And you would likely agree with the statement, "The Bible contains God's truth." On the surface, that sounds accurate. However, the statement is phrased that way for a reason. When someone says, "Oh, you know, the Bible contains the truth," they're framing the conversation in a way that enables them to talk about the things in the Bible that they don't believe are truth. They believe God can have His truth, and they can have theirs. They may argue, "Things have changed with culture." Or, "You don't understand. Jesus was deceived." They'll say things like, "Miracles don't exist." Or worse, "God doesn't exist."

So remember, the Bible doesn't only *contain* the truth; the Bible *is* the truth. All of it. Every word of it. From beginning to end.

To learn the truth, you've got to be in the Bible every day. Read it. Study it. Apply it. Be a diligent memorizer of it. There is no good reason for not reading your Bible every day.

I know there may be hindrances. For example, some people are dyslexic or can't read. Try listening to the Bible instead. We live in an amazing age; your phone can read it to you. Rely on others or new technology to help you meditate on God's Word. Let's not live for Jesus behind excuses. Good reasons can become bad excuses.

When you take in the Word of God, you're not only winning today but preparing for tomorrow. And when you're hiding God's Word in your heart, you carry it around with you all the time. It's your weapon.

Remember how Jesus faced the devil head-on? (Luke 4:1-13). The devil came to Him with partial truths that were full lies. How did Jesus defeat him? He quoted Scripture each time. And what did the devil do? He left. It's God's Word that will keep you wise and protect you in the spiritual battle.

John wrote, "I have written to you, fathers, because you have known Him who is from the beginning. I have written to you, young men, because you are strong, and the word of God abides in you, and you have overcome the wicked one" (1 John 2:14). How was the wicked one overcome? Because the Word of God abides in you.

You must read your Bible and pray every day. It's ammunition for the battle. Also, it's protective. It's absolutely needed. Don't let sad, sorry excuses hold you back from the power that lies in the truth. Every time you read God's Word, it's alive and powerful. It works inside you.

Now, I want to acknowledge that sometimes you'll read the Bible and you won't understand something. That is okay. For the time, skip that part. Write yourself a note: *I skipped Leviticus and details about God's laws for Israel. Come back later.* Please don't misunderstand me. Do not skip a passage in Scripture and never get back to it. Today, there are many things in the Bible that you will understand. Start by reading those passages, then return to the parts that are difficult. As you continue to grow in your knowledge, the Holy Spirit will continue to illuminate and bring you understanding of God's Word. And remember, God tells us in His Word that our ways and thoughts are not His (Isaiah 55:8-9). Some things we will not have a complete understanding of until we meet Him face to face.

If you are new to reading the Bible, here's my advice: Start in the New Testament and read the Gospel of John. The Gospel of John is easy to understand. Not only that, you'll read about the life of Jesus and get to know your Savior.

When you've finished the book of John, read Mark. The Gospel of Mark is another easy read. When you're done with Mark, read Luke. Then, read Matthew. The book of Matthew takes the prophecies and Scriptures of the Old Testament and shows you how Jesus fulfilled them. So the Gospel of Matthew can be challenging if you don't know the Old Testament. After you've read the Gospels, you can dive into the foundations of our faith from the Old Testament, or continue in the New Testament, reading about what God has revealed to His church for all time.

You can see how the enemy considers it advantageous to take the Word of God out of your hands, and he will try very hard to do so. He wants you to believe his lies and disregard the truth. Engaging with Scripture is hard. It is challenging. But God will give you the answers. You need the Word of God.

7. WE DEFEAT THE DEVIL BY PUTTING ON THE ARMOR OF GOD

God has given us spiritual armor for this spiritual war. In Ephesians 6, Paul wrote,

> My brethren, be strong in the Lord and in the power of His might. Put on the whole armor of God, that you may be able to stand against the wiles of the devil. For we do not wrestle against flesh and blood, but against principalities, against powers, against the rulers of the darkness of this age, against spiritual hosts of wickedness in the heavenly places. Therefore take up the whole armor of God, that you may be able to withstand in the evil day, and having done all, to stand (verses 10-13).

Remember, the word *stand* means to resist. *Stand* and *resist* have the same connotation. And that's God's will for you in the spiritual battle. He wants you to stand your ground. Don't give up an inch.

When Paul was writing his letter to the Ephesians, he was sitting in a Roman prison, chained to Roman guards. He utilized his circumstances as the backdrop for the imagery.

Ephesians 6 continues, "Stand therefore, having girded your waist with truth" (verse 14). First, we have the belt of truth, which is critically important. The belt—the truth—holds everything together. It's positioned under the rest of the armor but is necessary. If you don't have a belt, you're going to be exposed. You'll be vulnerable. If you don't have the truth, you'll be exposed to all sorts of lies. You need the belt of truth.

After girding your waist with truth, "put on the breastplate of righteousness" (verse 14). A breastplate was placed on the chest and covered the front of the body, the neck area, and the vital organs. It's God's righteousness that protects you and the vital aspects of your life. The breastplate of righteousness also protects your heart. In chapter 8, we discussed how the enemy attacks your emotions. When you remember what God has done for you and the righteousness He bestows upon you, you won't be as susceptible to your feelings. You've got to put on the breastplate of righteousness.

Next, "having shod your feet with the preparation of the gospel of peace" (verse 15), Paul wanted to prepare us to be ready to move. For a soldier, having the proper shoes is vital. They provide stability and mobility. The right shoes give a soldier the solid footing they need to fight the good fight. Here, the shoes are the gospel—the good news of what God has done for us.

Not only does the gospel protect you, but it also reminds you that wherever your feet go, you take the gospel with you. The gospel is the answer to every need for every person you meet. Deliverance comes when they cast their eyes on Jesus. You will effectively carry around the gospel if you've got your battle shoes on.

In verse 16, Paul listed, "Above all, taking the shield of faith with which you will be able to quench all the fiery darts of the wicked one." You might read that and think, *Wait a minute. Fiery darts?* Yes, the enemy has weapons of all sorts that he likes to use against us. And that includes arrows coming at you. Those darts are tipped with fire. When they hit their mark, a fire ignites. If an arrow strikes your depression, depression is set alight. If an arrow hits your identity, identity is inflamed. Whatever vulnerability the arrows hit, they ignite that one on fire.

To protect yourself, you must take up the shield of faith. A Roman shield was two feet wide by four feet high, a moveable wall that a soldier carried for protection from arrows. You can use the shield of faith to protect yourself from the enemy's fiery darts—the lies, the thoughts, and the doubts. The shield of faith will quench them. It will extinguish them.

In addition, during battle, as Roman armies advanced, soldiers would lock their shields together for more protection. We use this principle in the church. As a church, we lock shields. We go into the battle together. As we move forward, we protect ourselves and those beside us and behind us.

Another piece of armor that God has given us is the helmet of salvation (verse 17). The helmet of salvation protects your thinking. Your salvation—knowing who you are and what God is doing in your life—protects you against hopelessness and discouragement when the enemy attacks your mind with false thoughts.

God has also given us "the sword of the Spirit, which is the word of God" (verse 17). Paul's list of armor up to this point only included armor that is protective. But the sword of the Spirit is an offensive weapon. We discussed its instant effectiveness in battles with the devil in the previous point. The Word of God is a powerful sword.

Finally, in verse 18, Paul instructed us to use the armor while "praying always with all prayer and supplication in the Spirit, being watchful to this end with all perseverance and supplication for all the saints." Prayer is very important, which leads us to the eighth way to defeat the devil.

8. WE DEFEAT THE DEVIL WITH CONSTANT PRAYER

If you do not practice a habit of prayer in your life, you will remain weak. If there's no prayer surrounding your marriage, your marriage will be weak. If you don't pray with your kids, your family will be weak. It's the same in your singleness. Prayerlessness equals weakness. And when you are weak, you're vulnerable.

Prayer is a mighty weapon against the attacks of the enemy. Jesus shared about the importance of prayer. Luke 18:1 says that Jesus "spoke a parable to them, that men always ought to pray and not lose heart."

Prayer is a weapon that's available to all of us. You can pray even if your faith is weak, or you don't know much of the Bible. You can pray for yourself and for others. The real power we access in prayer is the Spirit. In Jude 20-21, the Bible tells us, "You, beloved, building yourselves up on your most holy faith, praying in the Holy Spirit, keep yourselves in the love of God, looking for the mercy of our Lord Jesus Christ unto eternal life." Praying in the Holy Spirit defeats the enemy.

In your prayer, you can intercede; ask, plead, and rest in God. As His child, you can bring your problems to Him and ask Him to take care of them.

Let me give you an example. Let's say your three-year-old son is playing in the bathroom. In whatever he was doing, he messed up the toilet, and it no longer works. When he comes to you and tells you what happened, do you reply, "Well, that's not my problem. Go and fix it. Call the plumber. Get your credit card out"? Of course not. No one would do that. If your small child messes up the toilet, who is going to fix it? You. Because you are their parent.

How much more will our heavenly Father take care of His kids? He shoulders the burden of the problem. We may have gotten ourselves into the mess and we may have contributed to it with our disobedience, but I'll tell you this: Your heavenly Father loves you and is ready to help you.

Go to Him in prayer. Talk to Him. Tell Him about your cares and concerns. Then, claim His promises. He promised to care for you, to watch over you, and to protect you. Prayer is a lifeline during challenging times.

In the final seven years of human history, soon after the rapture of the church, will be the great tribulation period. For those seven years, God will bring His judgment on a Christ-rejecting world. And God will turn His attention back to the nation of Israel to draw them to Himself.

During that cataclysmic time, there will be people who will get saved—the tribulation saints. They'll be genuine believers. And we have insight into what will give them their strength during the worst of times. Revelation 12:11 says, "They overcame [the accuser] by the blood of the Lamb and by the word of their testimony, and they did not love their lives to the death." The tribulation saints will be connected to God. The word of their testimony is the faithfulness of God, which they'll access through prayer.

/////

We are in the middle of a spiritual battle with the world, the flesh, and the devil. It's real. It's predictable. And, at times, it's overwhelming. It can take us by surprise and wear us down. Too often, we needlessly live in defeat.

But you don't need to live in a state of discouragement. You have defenses and weapons that God has given you to fight. Use them.

Don't give in. Don't collapse. Don't compromise. Don't run away. Don't depend on empty idols like the bottle or drugs. Don't run to streets where the world will wear you down. Don't aimlessly escape or wander away. Stand fast and fight. Fight the good fight.

Every time you take a stand for Jesus—every time you want to grow in Him and grow closer to Him—you can expect resistance. Great progress brings great resistance from the enemy. If you want to put these principles into practice, there will be times when you will get hit. It's going to be hard. Heavy spiritual warfare is a sign that you're on the right track.

So hold fast. Decide to obey. And remember: "'No weapon formed against you shall prosper, and every tongue which rises against you in judgment you shall condemn. This is the heritage of the servants of the LORD, and their righteousness is from Me,' says the LORD" (Isaiah 54:17).

REFLECTION/DISCUSSION QUESTIONS

1. We fight from a place of victory. How does this truth change your perspective on the trials and battles you face?
2. What does "resist the devil" (James 4:7) mean to you? What are some ways that you can practically apply this to your life?
3. Partial truths full of lies—in a world of half-truths and little white lies, how does this kind of thinking hinder your obedience and growth?
4. Which of the eight tactics for defeating the devil do you struggle with most? What strategies can you put in place to be more effective in this area?
5. Which piece of spiritual armor have you been neglecting? Why do you think this is? It is time to add it to your spiritual repertoire.

10

DEALING WITH YOUR IDENTITY

Do you know or do you recall the true story about Rahab the harlot? Before the Israelites crossed over the Jordan River, Joshua sent two men to check out the land that God had promised to them. Rahab hid the men so they would be safe from the king of Jericho. She knew that God had given the Israelites the land (Joshua 2).

Based on her faith, God ensured that Rahab and her family were saved when He brought down the wall of Jericho and delivered the city into the Israelites' hands (Joshua 6:22-23, 25). God redeemed Rahab. He even gave her the privilege of being in the genealogy of Jesus (Matthew 1:5).

There are times when you're reading through a passage of Scripture and something leaps off the page. There was a time when I was reading through the book of James and that happened to me. The passage read,

> Likewise, was not Rahab the harlot also justified by works when she received the messengers and sent them out another way? (James 2:25).

Three words stood out: *Rahab the harlot*. That's not the most endearing name to have. Wouldn't you agree? Rahab the harlot. Always remembered for her harlotry. And that's how she's known. Even generations later, James reminds us, this Rahab is the harlot that we read about in Joshua. Rahab the harlot. How sad.

But let us consider heaven. I wonder, *In heaven, will Rahab be known as Rahab the harlot?*

Think about it. All who are redeemed will be together in heaven. Imagine walking around meeting people whose lives are recorded in the Bible. Also, imagine trying to locate them. You say, "Hey, where's Abraham?" Others respond, "He's over there, that long line."

You don't want to wait in that line. So you ask, "Where's John the Baptist?" But you notice that line to talk with him is long too. Then you ask, "Where's Rahab the harlot?" And you hear, "There's no one by that name here."

There is no Rahab the harlot in heaven. She is Rahab the saint. She's Rahab the redeemed. She's Rahab the washed and cleansed. She is Rahab the changed life—one who loves Jesus. We won't identify people in heaven by their sin. We'll identify people by their Savior.

In the present, our tendency is to identify ourselves by our failures. Sometimes families can be like that, even if they're believers. They hold your past against you, even years later. You may be known by your failures—as the black sheep of the family. They may say things like, "Here comes you know who, the one who did you know what." You may even hold your failures against yourself, reminding yourself that you've always been the black sheep.

I know many of us struggle with our own feelings about people in our families. But may God convict us. Let us be compassionate with people in our families. Be patient with them. May the Lord help us not to identify people by their sin and by their failure, always holding the past up before them.

Let us consider heaven. Rahab's a saint. Rahab is no longer Rahab the harlot. Thomas isn't Thomas the doubter anymore. Peter isn't Peter the denier.

You're not defined by your sin either. You're identified by your Savior. In the eyes of God, you are seen as perfect in Christ. You are a new creation in Jesus (2 Corinthians 5:17). In Christ, you are clean (John 15:3) and complete (Colossians 2:10). You are righteous and holy (Ephesians 4:24). You are no longer defined by your sin.

Jesus has freed you and given you life. Because you've received liberty from Him, your faith does not need to be dead, useless, or lifeless. Instead, let your life bring glory and honor to God. As Jesus told us, "Let your light so shine before men, that they may see your good works and glorify your Father in heaven" (Matthew 5:16).

As you abide in Jesus, day by day and moment by moment, spend time meditating on the promises God has given you about who you are in Christ. As we've learned, if you are a born-again believer, you are in Christ. Remind yourself daily about who you are in Him.

But remember, God's promises about who you are in Christ are secondary to the God who keeps His promises. God's promises are great and wonderful. And our faith is in *God's* ability to keep His promises, not in *our* ability to remember them. Our faith is in the God who gives power, not in our ability to submit to Him. Our faith is in the God who does the work, not in our ability to recognize His work.

Did you know that God does a lot in your life that you don't even recognize? Even though you don't see it, He still loves you. Aren't you glad you're not saved by seeing everything that God does? God is doing things that He hasn't revealed to you yet. Your faith should be in God—not in what He does and not in what He gives. Your faith should be in *who* He is.

God's promises reveal His character and nature. That's where life is. Life is found in Jesus Christ. And it's conveyed to us from the inside out. Grace is amazing. A few minutes of Bible study doesn't even plumb the depths of the power of God in your life.

So as you think about who you are in Christ, remember that your position in Christ is based on God's ability to keep you there. Your position in Christ is not based on your ability to remember who you are in Christ. Even when you forget who you are in Christ, God's promises remain true. Our God is faithful (2 Timothy 2:13).

I do not have reflection/discussion questions for you in this chapter. Instead, following is a list of 90 ways that you are in Christ. Take time to think about these truths. Don't rush through them. Also, I challenge you to take a few months to go through the list. Each day, take a different truth and meditate on it. Soak in each one. Ask God to help you believe the promises He's given you about your nature as a born-again believer.

IN CHRIST:

1. You have been healed.

> He was wounded for our transgressions, He was bruised for our iniquities; the chastisement for our peace was upon Him, and by His stripes we are healed (Isaiah 53:5).

2. You are the salt of the earth.

> You are the salt of the earth; but if the salt loses its flavor, how shall it be seasoned? It is then good for nothing but to be thrown out and trampled underfoot by men (Matthew 5:13).

3. You are the light of the world.

> You are the light of the world. A city that is set on a hill cannot be hidden (Matthew 5:14).

4. You are commissioned to make disciples.

> Go therefore and make disciples of all the nations, baptizing them in the name of the Father and of the Son and of the Holy Spirit, teaching them to observe all things that

I have commanded you; and lo, I am with you always, even to the end of the age (Matthew 28:19-20).

5. You are a child of God.

As many as received Him, to them He gave the right to become children of God, to those who believe in His name (John 1:12).

6. You have eternal life.

My sheep hear My voice, and I know them, and they follow Me. And I give them eternal life, and they shall never perish; neither shall anyone snatch them out of My hand (John 10:27-28).

7. You have been given peace.

Peace I leave with you, My peace I give to you; not as the world gives do I give to you. Let not your heart be troubled, neither let it be afraid (John 14:27).

8. You are part of the true vine, a channel of Christ's life.

I am the true vine, and My Father is the vinedresser…I am the vine, you are the branches. He who abides in Me, and I in him, bears much fruit; for without Me you can do nothing (John 15:1, 5).

9. You are clean.

You are already clean because of the word which I have spoken to you (John 15:3).

10. You are Christ's friend.

No longer do I call you servants, for a servant does not know what his master is doing; but I have called you friends, for all things that I heard from My Father I have made known to you (John 15:15).

11. You have been chosen and appointed by Christ to bear His fruit.

You did not choose Me, but I chose you and appointed you that you should go and bear fruit, and that your fruit should remain, that whatever you ask the Father in My name He may give you (John 15:16).

12. You have been given glory.

The glory which You gave Me I have given them, that they may be one just as We are one (John 17:22).

13. You have been justified—completely forgiven and made righteous.

Having been justified by faith, we have peace with God through our Lord Jesus Christ (Romans 5:1).

14. You died with Christ and to the power of sin's rule over your life.

What shall we say then? Shall we continue in sin that grace may abound? Certainly not! How shall we who died to sin live any longer in it? Or do you not know that as many of us as were baptized into Christ Jesus were baptized into His death? Therefore we were buried with Him through baptism into death, that just as Christ was raised from the dead by the glory of the Father, even so we also should walk in newness of life. For if we have been united together in the likeness of His death, certainly we also shall be in the likeness of His resurrection, knowing this, that our old man was crucified with Him, that the body of sin might be done away with, that we should no longer be slaves of sin (Romans 6:1-6).

15. You are a slave of righteousness.

Having been set free from sin, you became slaves of righteousness (Romans 6:18).

16. You are free from sin and enslaved to God.

Now having been set free from sin, and having become slaves of God, you have your fruit to holiness, and the end, everlasting life (Romans 6:22).

17. You are free from condemnation forever.

There is therefore now no condemnation to those who are in Christ Jesus, who do not walk according to the flesh, but according to the Spirit (Romans 8:1).

18. You are a son or daughter of God; spiritually, God is your Father.

As many as are led by the Spirit of God, these are sons of God. For you did not receive the spirit of bondage again to fear, but you received the Spirit of adoption by whom we cry out, "Abba, Father" (Romans 8:14-15; see also Galatians 3:26; 4:6).

19. You are a joint heir with Christ, sharing His inheritance with Him.

The Spirit Himself bears witness with our spirit that we are children of God, and if children, then heirs—heirs of God and joint heirs with Christ, if indeed we suffer with Him, that we may also be glorified together (Romans 8:16-17).

20. You are more than a conqueror through Christ, who loves you.

In all these things we are more than conquerors through Him who loved us (Romans 8:37).

21. You have faith.

For I say, through the grace given to me, to everyone who is among you, not to think of himself more highly than he ought to think, but to think soberly, as God has dealt to each one a measure of faith (Romans 12:3).

22. You have been sanctified and called to holiness.

To the church of God which is at Corinth, to those who are sanctified in Christ Jesus, called to be saints, with all who in every place call on the name of Jesus Christ our Lord, both theirs and ours (1 Corinthians 1:2).

23. You have been given grace.

I thank my God always concerning you for the grace of God which was given to you by Christ Jesus (1 Corinthians 1:4).

24. You have been placed into Christ by God.

Of Him you are in Christ Jesus, who became for us wisdom from God—and righteousness and sanctification and redemption (1 Corinthians 1:30).

25. You have received God's Spirit so you might know the things that God has freely given you.

We have received, not the spirit of the world, but the Spirit who is from God, that we might know the things that have been freely given to us by God (1 Corinthians 2:12).

26. You have been given the mind of Christ.

For "who has known the mind of the LORD that he may instruct Him?" But we have the mind of Christ (1 Corinthians 2:16; see also Isaiah 40:13).

27. You are a temple—a dwelling place—of God, and His Spirit and life dwell in you.

Do you not know that you are the temple of God and that the Spirit of God dwells in you? (1 Corinthians 3:16; see also 1 Corinthians 6:19).

28. You are united to the Lord and are one spirit with Him.

He who is joined to the Lord is one spirit with Him (1 Corinthians 6:17).

29. You have been bought with a price; you are not your own; you belong to God.

Do you not know that your body is the temple of the Holy Spirit who is in you, whom you have from God, and you are not your own? For you were bought at a price; therefore glorify God in your body and in your spirit, which are God's (1 Corinthians 6:19-20; see also 1 Corinthians 7:23).

30. You are called.

As God has distributed to each one, as the Lord has called each one, so let him walk. And so I ordain in all the churches (1 Corinthians 7:17).

31. You are a member of Christ's body.

You are the body of Christ, and members individually (1 Corinthians 12:27; see also Ephesians 5:30).

32. You are victorious through Jesus Christ.

Thanks be to God, who gives us the victory through our Lord Jesus Christ (1 Corinthians 15:57).

33. You have been established, anointed, and sealed by God; God gave you the Holy Spirit as a pledge that guarantees your inheritance to come.

He who establishes us with you in Christ and has anointed us is God (2 Corinthians 1:21; see also Ephesians 1:13-14).

34. You are led by God in a triumphal procession.

Thanks be to God who always leads us in triumph in Christ, and through us diffuses the fragrance of His knowledge in every place (2 Corinthians 2:14).

35. You are, to God, the fragrance of Christ among those who are being saved.

We are to God the fragrance of Christ among those who are being saved and among those who are perishing (2 Corinthians 2:15).

36. You are being changed into the likeness of Christ.

We all, with unveiled face, beholding as in a mirror the glory of the Lord, are being transformed into the same image from glory to glory, just as by the Spirit of the Lord (2 Corinthians 3:18).

37. You no longer live for yourself since you have died, but for Christ.

The love of Christ compels us, because we judge thus: that if One died for all, then all died; and He died for all, that those who live should live no longer for themselves, but for Him who died for them and rose again (2 Corinthians 5:14-15).

38. You are a new creation.

If anyone is in Christ, he is a new creation; old things have passed away; behold, all things have become new (2 Corinthians 5:17).

39. You are reconciled to God and a minister of reconciliation.

All things are of God, who has reconciled us to Himself through Jesus Christ, and has given us the ministry of reconciliation, that is, that God was in Christ reconciling the world to Himself, not imputing their trespasses to them, and has committed to us the word of reconciliation (2 Corinthians 5:18-19).

40. You have been made righteous.

He made Him who knew no sin to be sin for us, that we might become the righteousness of God in Him (2 Corinthians 5:21).

41. You have been given strength in exchange for your weakness.

I take pleasure in infirmities, in reproaches, in needs, in persecutions, in distresses, for Christ's sake. For when I am weak, then I am strong (2 Corinthians 12:10).

42. You have been crucified with Christ; it is no longer you who live but Christ who lives in you.

I have been crucified with Christ; it is no longer I who live, but Christ lives in me; and the life which I now live in the flesh I live by faith in the Son of God, who loved me and gave Himself for me (Galatians 2:20).

43. You are a son or daughter of God and one in Christ.

You are all sons of God through faith in Christ Jesus... There is neither Jew nor Greek, there is neither slave nor free, there is neither male nor female; for you are all one in Christ Jesus (Galatians 3:26, 28).

44. You are Abraham's seed and an heir of the promise.

If you are Christ's, then you are Abraham's seed, and heirs according to the promise (Galatians 3:29).

45. You are an heir of God because you are a son or daughter of God.

Because you are sons, God has sent forth the Spirit of His Son into your hearts, crying out, "Abba, Father!" Therefore you are no longer a slave but a son, and if a son, then an heir of God through Christ (Galatians 4:6-7).

46. You are a saint.

Paul, an apostle of Jesus Christ by the will of God, to the saints who are in Ephesus, and faithful in Christ Jesus (Ephesians 1:1; see also 1 Corinthians 1:2; Philippians 1:1; Colossians 1:2).

47. You have been blessed with every spiritual blessing.

Blessed be the God and Father of our Lord Jesus Christ, who has blessed us with every spiritual blessing in the heavenly places in Christ (Ephesians 1:3).

48. You were chosen before the foundation of the world to be holy; you are without blame before God.

Just as He chose us in Him before the foundation of the world, that we should be holy and without blame before Him in love (Ephesians 1:4).

49. You were predestined—determined by God—to be adopted as His child.

Having predestined us to adoption as sons by Jesus Christ to Himself, according to the good pleasure of His will (Ephesians 1:5).

50. You have been sealed with the Holy Spirit.

In Him you also trusted, after you heard the word of truth, the gospel of your salvation; in whom also, having believed, you were sealed with the Holy Spirit of promise (Ephesians 1:13).

51. You have been redeemed and forgiven; you are a recipient of God's lavish grace.

God, who is rich in mercy, because of His great love with which He loved us (Ephesians 2:4).

52. You have been made alive together with Christ.

Even when we were dead in trespasses, [God] made us alive together with Christ (by grace you have been saved) (Ephesians 2:5).

53. You have been raised up and seated with Christ in heaven.

[God] raised us up together, and made us sit together in the heavenly places in Christ Jesus (Ephesians 2:6).

54. You are God's workmanship—His handiwork—born anew in Christ to do His work.

We are His workmanship, created in Christ Jesus for good works, which God prepared beforehand that we should walk in them (Ephesians 2:10).

55. You have direct access to God through the Spirit.

Through Him we both have access by one Spirit to the Father (Ephesians 2:18).

56. You are a fellow citizen among the rest of God's family.

You are no longer strangers and foreigners, but fellow citizens with the saints and members of the household of God (Ephesians 2:19).

57. You may approach God with boldness, freedom, and confidence.

In [Christ] we have boldness and access with confidence through faith in Him (Ephesians 3:12).

58. You are righteous and holy.

Put on the new man which was created according to God, in true righteousness and holiness (Ephesians 4:24).

59. You are a citizen of heaven and your residence is secure.

Our citizenship is in heaven, from which we also eagerly wait for the Savior, the Lord Jesus Christ (Philippians 3:20; see also Ephesians 2:6).

60. You are capable.

I can do all things through Christ who strengthens me (Philippians 4:13).

61. You have been rescued from the domain of Satan's rule and transferred to the kingdom of Christ.

He has delivered us from the power of darkness and conveyed us into the kingdom of the Son of His love (Colossians 1:13).

62. You have been redeemed and forgiven of all your sins; the debt you owed has been canceled.

In [God's Son] we have redemption through His blood, the forgiveness of sins (Colossians 1:14).

63. You are blameless and free from accusation.

[Christ] has reconciled in the body of His flesh through death, to present you holy, and blameless, and above reproach in His sight (Colossians 1:21-22).

64. You are indwelt by Christ Himself.

To them God willed to make known what are the riches of the glory of this mystery among the Gentiles: which is Christ in you, the hope of glory (Colossians 1:27).

65. You are firmly rooted in Christ and are being built up by Him.

Rooted and built up in Him and established in the faith, as you have been taught, abounding in it with thanksgiving (Colossians 2:7).

66. You have been made complete.

You are complete in Him, who is the head of all principality and power (Colossians 2:10).

67. You have been spiritually circumcised; your old, unregenerate nature has been removed.

In Him you were also circumcised with the circumcision made without hands, by putting off the body of the sins of the flesh, by the circumcision of Christ (Colossians 2:11).

68. You have been buried, raised, and made alive with Christ.

Buried with Him in baptism, in which you also were raised with Him through faith in the working of God, who raised Him from the dead. And you, being dead in your trespasses and the uncircumcision of your flesh, He has made alive together with Him, having forgiven you all trespasses (Colossians 2:12-13).

69. You died with Christ and have been raised up with Him; your life is now hidden with Christ in God.

If then you were raised with Christ, seek those things which are above, where Christ is, sitting at the right hand of God. Set your mind on things above, not on things on the earth. For you died, and your life is hidden with Christ in God (Colossians 3:1-3).

70. You are an expression of Christ's life because He is your life.

When Christ who is our life appears, then you also will appear with Him in glory (Colossians 3:4).

71. You are chosen by God, holy, and dearly loved.

As the elect of God, holy and beloved, put on tender mercies, kindness, humility, meekness, longsuffering (Colossians 3:12).

72. You are a son or daughter of light and not of darkness.

You are all sons of light and sons of the day. We are not of the night nor of darkness (1 Thessalonians 5:5).

73. You have been given a spirit of power, love, and self-discipline.

God has not given us a spirit of fear, but of power and of love and of a sound mind (2 Timothy 1:7).

74. You have been saved and set apart by God.

[God] who has saved us and called us with a holy calling, not according to our works, but according to His own purpose and grace which was given to us in Christ Jesus before time began (2 Timothy 1:9; see also Titus 3:5).

75. Jesus is not ashamed to call you His brother or sister because you are sanctified and one with the Sanctifier.

Both He who sanctifies and those who are being sanctified are all of one, for which reason He is not ashamed to call them brethren (Hebrews 2:11).

76. You are a holy partaker of a heavenly calling.

Holy brethren, partakers of the heavenly calling, consider the Apostle and High Priest of our confession, Christ Jesus (Hebrews 3:1).

77. You have the right to come boldly before God's throne to find mercy and grace in a time of need.

Let us therefore come boldly to the throne of grace, that we may obtain mercy and find grace to help in time of need (Hebrews 4:16).

78. You have been born again.

Having been born again, not of corruptible seed but incorruptible, through the word of God which lives and abides forever (1 Peter 1:23).

79. You are one of God's living stones, being built up in Christ as a spiritual house.

You also, as living stones, are being built up a spiritual house, a holy priesthood, to offer up spiritual sacrifices acceptable to God through Jesus Christ (1 Peter 2:5).

80. You are a member of a chosen race, a royal priesthood, a holy nation, and a people for God's own possession.

You are a chosen generation, a royal priesthood, a holy nation, His own special people, that you may proclaim the praises of Him who called you out of darkness into His marvelous light; who once were not a people but are now the people of God, who had not obtained mercy but now have obtained mercy (1 Peter 2:9-10).

81. You are an alien and stranger of this world in which you temporarily live.

Beloved, I beg you as sojourners and pilgrims, abstain from fleshly lusts which war against the soul (1 Peter 2:11).

82. You are an enemy of the devil.

Be sober, be vigilant; because your adversary the devil walks about like a roaring lion, seeking whom he may devour (1 Peter 5:8; see also John 10:10).

83. You have been given exceedingly great and precious promises by God, by which you are a partaker of God's divine nature.

[God has] given to us exceedingly great and precious promises, that through these you may be partakers of the divine nature, having escaped the corruption that is in the world through lust (2 Peter 1:4).

84. You are forgiven on account of Jesus' name.

I write to you, little children, because your sins are forgiven you for His name's sake (1 John 2:12).

85. You are anointed by God.

The anointing which you have received from Him abides in you, and you do not need that anyone teach you; but as the same anointing teaches you concerning all things, and is true, and is not a lie, and just as it has taught you, you will abide in Him (1 John 2:27).

86. You are a child of God, and you will resemble Christ when He returns.

Behold what manner of love the Father has bestowed on us, that we should be called children of God! Therefore the world does not know us, because it did not know Him. Beloved, now we are children of God; and it has not yet been revealed what we shall be, but we know that when He is revealed, we shall be like Him, for we shall see Him as He is (1 John 3:1-2).

87. You are loved.

In this is love, not that we loved God, but that He loved us and sent His Son to be the propitiation for our sins (1 John 4:10).

88. You have life.

He who has the Son has life; he who does not have the Son of God does not have life (1 John 5:12).

89. You are born of God, and the evil one—the devil—cannot touch you.

We know that whoever is born of God does not sin; but he who has been born of God keeps himself, and the wicked one does not touch him (1 John 5:18).

90. You have been redeemed.

They sang a new song, saying: "You are worthy to take the scroll, and to open its seals; for You were slain, and have redeemed us to God by Your blood out of every tribe and tongue and people and nation, and have made us kings and priests to our God; and we shall reign on the earth" (Revelation 5:9).

AFTERWORD

Friend, I know dealing with your past will include more than simply reading this book. It's not a task that is as straightforward as some people think. However, after what we have discussed, I pray that you will find it to be easier than you felt before. God is ready to work on your behalf right now!

I know that God will use this book, and the things you've learned, to release you from those things that hold you in bondage. As you choose to put these principles into practice, you will begin to experience the life you've always wanted to live.

It will not be easy. There will be setbacks. Keep making those forward-facing decisions that God will honor with the power and presence of His Holy Spirit.

If you need prayer, you can email me directly at ed@edtaylor.org.

May the Lord bless you and strengthen you for the battle!

> For this reason I bow my knees to the Father of our Lord Jesus Christ, from whom the whole family in heaven and earth is named, that He would grant you, according to the riches of His glory, to be strengthened with might through His Spirit in the inner man, that Christ may dwell in your hearts through faith; that you, being rooted and grounded

in love, may be able to comprehend with all the saints what is the width and length and depth and height—to know the love of Christ which passes knowledge; that you may be filled with all the fullness of God.

Now to Him who is able to do exceedingly abundantly above all that we ask or think, according to the power that works in us, to Him be glory in the church by Christ Jesus to all generations, forever and ever. Amen (Ephesians 3:14-21).

NOTES

CHAPTER 2—DEALING WITH CONDEMNATION

1. *Merriam-Webster's Dictionary*, s.v. "condemn (*v.*)," accessed January 27, 2023, https://www.merriam-webster.com/dictionary/condemn.

CHAPTER 3—DEALING WITH THE LAW OF GOD

1. Olive Tree Bible Software, ed., *Olive Tree Enhanced Strong's Dictionary* (n.p.: Olive Tree, 2011), *koper*, Strong's number H3724 ("price of a life, ransom").
2. Olive Tree, *Enhanced Strong's Dictionary*, *kapar*, Strong's number H3722.

CHAPTER 4—DEALING WITH YOUR PAST

1. Olive Tree, *Enhanced Strong's Dictionary*, *dioko*, Strong's number G1377.
2. Olive Tree, *Enhanced Strong's Dictionary*, *rahaq*, Strong's number H7368.

CHAPTER 5—DEALING WITH FORGIVENESS

1. This story is based on a local tale told in Madrid that is also found in Ernest Hemingway's short story *The Capital of the World.* Ernest Hemingway, "The Capital of the World," in *The First Forty-Nine Stories* (London: Jonathan Cape, 1946), 44.
2. Craig Caster, *Forgiveness and Reconciliation Workbook* (El Cajon, CA: Family Discipleship Ministries, 2013). Used with permission.
3. Olive Tree, *Enhanced Strong's Dictionary*, *katartizo*, Strong's number G2675.

CHAPTER 6—DEALING WITH YOUR ANGER

1. Theopedia, s.v. "Anger," accessed February 2, 2023, https://www.theopedia.com/anger.
2. Mayumi Okuda, et al., "Prevalence and Correlates of Anger in the Community: Results from a National Survey," National Center for Biotechnology Information (April 1, 2016), https://www.ncbi.nlm.nih.gov/pmc/ articles/PMC4384185/.

3. Mayo Clinic Staff, "Anger Management: 10 tips to tame your temper," Mayo Clinic, accessed January 28, 2023, https://www.mayoclinic.org/healthy-lifestyle/adult-health/in-depth/anger-management/art-20045434; Kimberly Holland, "How to Control Anger: 25 Tips to Help You Stay Calm," Healthline (January 29, 2019), https://www.healthline.com/health/mental-health/how-to-control-anger; Dan Mager, "8 Strategies to Work Through Anger and Resentment," *Psychology Today* (January 17, 2017), https://www.psychologytoday.com/us/blog/some-assembly-required/201701/8-strategies-work-through-anger-and-resentment.
4. Mayo Clinic Staff, "Anger Management: 10 tips to tame your temper," Mayo Clinic, accessed January 28, 2023, https://www.mayoclinic.org/healthy-lifestyle/adult-health/in-depth/anger-management/art-20045434.
5. "Anger—Shotgun," Bible.org, accessed January 28, 2023, https://bible.org/illustration/anger-shotgun.

CHAPTER 7—DEALING WITH THE PRESENT

1. Olive Tree, *Enhanced Strong's Dictionary*, *meno*, Strong's number G3306.
2. Ronald F. Youngblood, ed., *Nelson's New Illustrated Bible Dictionary* (Nashville, TN: Thomas Nelson, Inc., 1995), s.v. "Pharisees."